PROVERBS,
EAST *and* WEST

PROVERBS,
EAST *and* WEST

An Anthology of
Chinese, Korean, and Japanese Sayings
with Western Equivalents

COMPILED BY
KIM YONG-CHOL

HOLLYM

First published by Hollym International Corp.
18 Donald Place, Elizabeth, New Jersey 07208 U.S.A.
Phone: (908)353-1655   Fax: (908)353-0255

Published simultaneously in Korea
by Hollym Corporation; Publishers
14-5 Kwanchol-dong, Chongno-gu, Seoul, Korea
Phone: (02)735-7554   Fax: (02)730-5149

ISBN: 0-930878-09-4
Library of Congress Catalog Card Number: 91-72180

Drawings by Hyunjoo Lee
Printed in Korea

The People's Voice the Voice of God we calll;
And what are proverbs but the People's Voice?
— *James Howell*

The genius, wit, and spirit of a nation are
discovered in its proverbs. — *Francis Bacon*

Maxims are the condensed good sense of
nations. — *Sir James Mackintosh*

The proverbs of a nation furnish the index to
its spirit. — *J. G. Holland*

Judge a country by the quality of its proverbs.
— *German proverb*

PREFACE

THIS BOOK is a personal selection of proverbial sayings deriving from the peoples of China, Korea, and Japan, three kindred nations of the Far East. One of the chief features of this book is that it presents the selected proverbs of those three nations in one compendious volume so that the reader may see them with a comparatist's eye. A total of 1,359 Asian proverbs in English translation have been chosen for the book — 549 Chinese, 404 Korean, and 406 Japanese. The nationality of each Asian proverb is indicated by a letter: [C] for Chinese, [K] for Korean, and [J] for Japanese. When proverbs of the three Asian nations fall under a single thematic category, a Chinese proverb is placed first, a Korean proverb next, and then a Japanese proverb. This reflects the historical eastward flow of Chinese culture through the Korean Peninsula to Japan.

Another important feature of this book is that it places each group of Asian proverbs with a comparable group of Western proverbs so that the reader may view the Asian proverbs against their Western equivalents. As many as 867 Western proverbs have been chosen for this book; the majority of them are proverbs of England and America. The nationality of each Western proverb is not given.

This book is not intended to be used as a dictionary, though many collections of proverbs are so designed; it is meant to be read for sheer enjoyment and contemplation. To help promote that objective, I have arranged the proverbs in topical categories, ranging from Anger to Wisdom. Whenever a category warrants it, I have divided the category into smaller groups. Thus, love is sub-categorized into its power, its blindness, its rules and conditions, its pleasure and pain, love and hate, and parental love.

As for the arrangement of the thematic categories themselves, I have not chosen the usual alphabetical arrangement, but, again to make the book more thought provoking, I have grouped the thematic categories into nine larger themes, constituting the titles of the nine chapters in the book. The sequence in which the chapters are arranged is rather subjective, but every effort has been made to cover as much of the whole domain of morals and manners as possible.

An introductory comment is provided at the outset of each chapter to enable the reader to view the chapter theme in its socio-cultural perspectives. Explanatory notes have been provided for a good number of Asian proverbs whose meanings would seem ambiguous to Western readers. Each chapter concludes with a small cluster of aphorisms from authors of many nations. Less homely and practical than many common proverbs, these aphorisms often parody the popular platitudes that many proverbs offer. Thus, at each chapter's end the reader will reflect upon the double edges and dichotomies at work in human thoughts and feelings.

An index of key words and concepts is provided at the back of the book. Arranged alphabetically, this index will help the reader to approach the proverbs from other perspectives. There is also provided an index of the Western proverbs presented in this book. By using it, a Western reader may locate Asian proverbs through Western proverbs already familiar to him.

K. Y. C.

ACKNOWLEDGMENTS

AS DO many compilers and editors of proverbs, I owe a considerable debt to previous collections and anthologies in the field. First of all, with the help of S. G. Champion's *Racial Proverbs* (1938) I was able to undertake an arduous but profitable journey into the proverbs of diverse nations in the world. (When Champion was putting out his first edition, Korea was under Japanese control, and so only a limited number of Korean proverbs were listed, in the Japanese section at that.)

In the area of Asian proverbs, I am indebted to the following.

Chinese

William Scarborough, trans. and arr., *A Collection of Chinese Proverbs*. Shanghai, 1875.

Chian Ker Chiu, *Chinese Proverbs in Romanised Mandarin and Cantonese with English Literal Translation, Explanation and Foot Notes*. Singapore, n.d.

William H. Bueler, comp., *Chinese Sayings*. Rutland, Vt. and Tokyo, 1972.

C. C. Sun, *As the Saying Goes: An Annotated Anthology of Chinese and Equivalent English Sayings and Expressions*. St. Lucia, 1981.

Korean

Ki Mun Lee, ed., *Dictionary of Korean Proverbs*. Seoul, 1962. (Exclusively in Korean)

Tae Hung Ha, ed., *Maxims and Proverbs of Old Korea*. Seoul, 1964.

Bruce K. Grant, ed., *Korean Proverbs*. Salt Lake City

and Seoul, 1982.

Jung Young Lee, ed., *Sokdam: Capsules of Korean Wisdom.* Seoul, 1983.

Dennis Dunham, ed., *Proverbs in Korean and English.* Seoul, 1986.

Japanese

Aisaburo Akiyama, ed., *Japanese Proverbs and Proverbial Phrases.* Kyoto, 1935.

Daniel Buchanan, ed., *Japanese Proverbs and Sayings,* Norman, Oklahoma, 1965.

Fumio Okutsu, *English and Japanese Proverbs: A Comparative Study.* Tokyo, 1978.

Taiji Takashima, ed., *Fountain of Japanese Proverbs.* Tokyo, 1981.

Yasaburo Ikeda and Donald Keene, eds., *Proverbs: Dictionary of Proverbs in Japanese and English.* Tokyo, 1982.

In addition, for Chinese and Japanese proverbs in English translation, Justin Wintle's recent anthology, *The Dragon's Almanac: Chinese and Japanese and Other Far Eastern Proverbs* was consulted. Wakamatsu Mi's *Glossary of Japanese Proverbs in Korean* was extremely useful in seeing the close relationships between the proverbs of both countries.

In the area of Western proverbs, I am indebted to the following.

William George Smith, comp., *The Oxford Dictionary of English Proverbs.* Oxford, 1935.

Burton Stevenson, ed., *The Home Book of Proverbs, Maxims and Familiar Phrases.* New York, 1948.

A. Jonson, *Common English Proverbs.* London and New York, 1954.

David Kin, ed., *Dictionary of American Proverbs.* New
York, 1955.

V. H. Collins, *A Book of English Proverbs with Origins
and Explanations.* London and New York, 1959.

J. A. Simpson, ed., *The Concise Oxford Dictionary of
Proverbs.* Oxford, 1982.

Rosalind Fergusson, comp., *The Facts of File Dictionary
of Proverbs.* New York, 1983.

In the area of aphorisms and quotations, I am indebted
to the following.

H. L. Mencken, ed., *A New Dictionary of Quotations
on Historical Principles from Ancient and Modern
Sources.* New York, 1942.

Rodolph Flesch, ed., *The Book of Unusual Quotations.*
New York, 1957.

Bergen Evans, ed., *Dictionary of Quotations.* New
York, 1968.

W. H. Auden and Louis Kronenberger, eds., *The Vi-
king Book of Aphorisms.* New York, 1962.

John Gross, ed., *The Oxford Book of Aphorisms.* New
York, 1983.

I am grateful to Sung Kyun Kwan University in Seoul
for granting me a leave of absence, during which time I
was able to do the sustained work required to complete
this book. I am also grateful to the Center for Korean
Studies, University of California at Berkeley, for granting
me the privilege of utilizing the library facilities and other
valuable resources at the university. I must also extend my
thanks to Mr. Insoo Rhimm, president of Hollym
Publishers, to Mr. Shinwon Chu, vice president, and to
Miss Kyoung-hee Uhm, editor, for their professional advice and assistance. I cannot sufficiently thank Professor

John Holstein of Sung Kyun Kwan University for his editorial advice. Last but not least, my warm thanks are due to my family: to my wife Jae who abided through this project with proverbial Oriental patience, to my children Helen, Angie, Joe, and Sophie, who have been unfailing supporters of my project all along, and to my son-in-law Ted and my daughter-in-law Meeky and our family friend Mark, who encouraged me with their sympathetic interest. Especially, my son Joe and my daughter Sophie re-energized my drooping spirits, sometimes with many hours of talk on this project, sometimes with prompt material assistance.

Contents

CHAPTER ONE

The Virtues

THROUGH ALL ages many nations and cultures have celebrated themselves on the positive traits of human character. These traits, they thought, made a man generous, sympathetic, courageous, fair-minded, wise, or simply admirable in character and conduct. This section, treating of various aspects of those inner qualities, illustrates the three Asian nations' widened but keen interest in good morals and proper ways of living. The Western nations and cultures, whose proverbs and maxims are represented here, are equally keen in their attention to the art of enlightened living.

1 VIRTUE

Virtue: its nature

1   Riches adorn the dwelling; virtue adorns the person.
[C]

2   The virtuous mind is serene as a granite mountain. [J]

3   No poverty where virtue is; no riches where virtue is
not.   [C]

4   He who is stout-hearted and daring is a man of virtue.
[J]

5   Virtue carries a lean purse.   [J]

6   Virtue never dwells alone, it always has neighbors.
[C] [K]

7   Beneath the wisdom and courage of all great men lies
the heart of a little child.   [C]

8   A truly great man never puts away the simplicity of a
child.   [C]

9   The heart of a little child is like the heart of Buddha.
[C]

10 A heart like silk brocade. [K]

11 Rather than dream of jade and gold, pray for virtue among your children and grandchildren. [C]

12 Be like the tree which covers with its blossoms the hand that shakes it. [J]

13 A good heart always gives a little extra. [C]

Western Equivalents

14 Virtue is the beauty of the mind.

15 Virtue is a jewel of great price.

16 Virtue and a trade are the best portion for children.

17 Virtue is the only true nobility.

18 A good heart conquers ill fortune.

19 A good heart cannot lie.

Doing good

20 Follow goodness as constantly as a river follows its bed. [J]

21 The pleasure of doing good never wears out. [C]

22 Practice good deeds with no thought of benefit. [C]

23 When doing good works, let no one best you. [C]

24   Live with a good heart, and you will turn into a good spirit when you depart from this world.   **[K]**

† In old Korea, people believed that a man turns at his death into a good or a bad spirit.

25   Keep your heart pure, and the Big Dipper will smile on you.   **[K]**

26   Better is one good deed than three days of fasting at a shrine.   **[J]**

27   One good deed atones for a thousand bad ones.   **[C]**

28   Being good brings good reward.   **[C]**

29   To see a man do a good deed is to forget all his faults.   **[C]**

Western Equivalents

30   Follow virtue like its shadow.

31   Do well and have well.

32   Virtue is its own reward.

33   He that does well wearies not himself.

34   One good turn deserves another.

35   He dies like a beast who has done no good while he lived.

36   They die well that live well.

37   A house is a fine house when good folks are within.

38   He that walketh with the virtuous is one of them.

*   *   *

Virtue debases itself in justifying itself.
                                        — *Francois Voltaire*

There is no greater injury to one's character than
practicing virtue with motivation.
                                        — *Chuang-tzu*

To many people virtue consists chiefly in repenting
faults, not in avoiding them.
                                        — *G. C. Lichtenberg*

Virtue is the trunk of man's nature, and music is
the blossoming of virtue.
                                        — *Confucius*

2 KINDNESS

Kindness as fellow feelings

39   It is always good to travel with a friend, but on life's
      journey travel with kindness.   [*C*]

40   On a journey, a fellow traveler; on a journey of life,
      fellow feelings.   [*J*]

[38—40]

4¹ In consuming itself a candle gives light to others. [*J*]

4² It is the poor who give alms to the poor. [*J*]

4³ Of opposing warriors, he who has pity conquers. [*C*]

44 Love grows out of pity or sympathy. [*C*]

In consuming itself a candle gives light to others.

45 Better a kind friend than an unkind brother. [C]

46 There is no sword against kindness. [J]

47 Even a thief can show a kind heart. [K]

Western Equivalents

48 He is a god that helps a man.

49 The sea refuses no river.

50 Kindness comes of will, it cannot be bought.

51 Kindness is the noblest weapon to conquer with.

52 Pity is akin to love.

53 Pity is but one remove from love.

54 Pity swells the tide of love.

55 Charity covers a multitude of sins.

Kindness as a social virtue

56 Behave toward everyone as if receiving a great guest.
[C]

57 Treat every old man as thy father. [J]

58 Those obliged to bow should bow low. [C]

59 He who bows never gets slapped on the cheek. [K]

60 Much courtesy forestalls offence. [C]

61 Being polite means taking nothing amiss. [C]

62 Every intimacy should be attended by courtesy. [J]

63 Even a sage follows the customs of the times. [K]

64 When the son stands and the father sits, true courtesy is shown. [C]

Western Equivalents

65 Civility costs nothing.

66 Courtesy is the inseparable companion of virtue.

67 He that asketh a courtesy promiseth a kindness.

68 A courtesy is a flower.

69 Do on the hill as you would do in the hall.

Acts of kindness

70 Do continually deeds of kindness; perform every sort of secret virtue. [C]

71 He who distributes charcoal during a snowstorm is truly a superior man. [C]

72 Always leave a way of escape to the erring. [C]

73 Deal with the faults of others as gently as you do your own. [C]

74 A good heart always gives a little extra. [C]

[61−74]

75 There is more credit in saving one man's life than in building a seven-tiered pagoda. [C]

76 Kindness at home is better than burning incense in remote places. [C]

77 Better to feed the hungry than to offer alms to Buddha. [K]

78 To make a new dress for the beggar. [K]

† A man doing a good deed like this is so good in character that he expects no reward.

79 To conduct a blind man over the bridge. [J]

80 To others be indulgent, but not to yourself. [J]

81 Requite the evil deed with a good one. [J]

Western Equivalents

82 Charity begins at home.

83 Never forget a kindness.

84 It is a kindly act to help the fallen.

85 He that plants trees love others besides himself.

86 He that pities another remembers himself.

87 He gives twice who gives quickly.

Gratitude: the other side of kindness

88   He who is one day my teacher is my father for life.
[C]

89   When you drink from the stream, remember the
spring.   [C]

90   When eating a bamboo shoot, remember him who
grew it.   [C]

91   You may forget the favors you gave, but remember
the blessings you received.   [C]

92   Do not forget little kindnesses, nor remember little
faults.   [C]

93   Feed a dog for five days, and he will begin to
appreciate your kindness.   [K]

† The implication is that many ungrateful human beings
are morally inferior even to a dog, which seems to
know how to show gratitude.

94   Feed a dog for three days, and he will remember
your kindness for three years.   [J]

† Synonymous with #93.

95   You can never appreciate your parents' love until you
have a child of your own.   [J]

Western Equivalents

96   God and parents and our masters can never be
requited.

97 Without taste, without gratitude.

98 Gratitude is the memory of the heart.

99 Gratitude and wheat only grow on good ground.

100 You may believe any good of a grateful man.

A kindness rewarded

101 Oblige, and you will be obliged. [C]

102 Being good brings good reward. [C]

103 In accommodating others you accommodate yourself. [C]

104 The rivers pour their waters back again into the sea; what a man lends is returned to him again. [C]

105 If fish are kind-hearted, water is also kind-hearted. [J]

106 A kindness is given before it is returned. [K]

107 Your goodwill toward others returns to yourself in the end. [J]

108 If you do not want people to grind their teeth at you, do not knit your brows at them. [C]

109 If you want to get on in the world, first help others to get on. [J]

Western Equivalents

110 One kindness is the price of another.

111 One good turn deserves another.

112 The hand that gives, gathers.

113 Claw me and I will claw thee.

114 Scratch my back and I'll scratch yours.

115 He who is grateful for a kindness unlocks the door for another.

Kindnesses wasted

116 Save a traveler from drowning, and he'll turn and demand his baggage. [K]

117 A kindness to a starfish is like a gust of wind in the desert. [J]

118 Too much courtesy is a discourtesy. [J]

119 To be kind enough to give a stray dog a rice ball. [J]

† A stray dog is generally considered ungrateful, so a kindness shown to the dog is most likely wasted.

Western Equivalents

120 Nothing ages so quickly as a kindness.

121 Give a clown your finger, and he will take your hand.

122   Give him an inch and he will take a yard.

123   Kindness to the just is never lost, but kindness to the wicked is unkindness to yourself.

124   The hog never looks up to him that threshes down the acorns.

*   *   *

To cultivate kindness is a valuable part of the business of life.

— *Samuel Johnson*

When kindness has left people, even for a few moments, we become afraid of them, as if their reason had left them.

— *Willa Cather*

Because I am merciful, I can be brave.... For heaven will come to the rescue of the merciful and protect him with *its* mercy.

— *Lao-tzu*

3 LOVE

Love: its power

125   Love is an inscrutable monster.   [*J*]

126   Love and leprosy few escape.   [C]

127   No medicine to cure love sickness.   [J]

128   To a lover a thousand miles are only ten miles.   [K]

  † The unit of distance in the original language is
  actually *ri*, but the word "mile" is used here for the
  Western reader's ease of perception.

129   To a lover going to and fro, a thousand miles are but
      one.   [J]

130   The heart surrendered at first sight.   [C]

131   The butterfly that spots the flower he loves never
      reckons with the risks of fire.   [K]

132   The butterfly that spots the flower he loves never
      flies away over the hedge.   [K]

Western Equivalents

133   To those in love miles are only paces.

134   He who has love in his heart has spurs in his heels.

135   There is no physician or physic for love.

136   Love will go through stone walls.

137   Love makes all hard hearts gentle.

138   A man has the choice to begin love, but not to end
      it.

To a lover a thousand miles are only ten miles.

Love: its blindness

139   **A "blind" love.**   **[K]**

140   **In the eyes of the lover, a pockmark's a dimple.**   **[J]**

141   **The harelip is taken for a dimple.**   **[J]**

142   **Every man has his own Yang Chi.**   **[C]**

> † Yang Chi was a beautiful princess of ancient China. The implication here is that every man thinks his wife or sweetheart is as beautiful as Yang Chi.

143   **To the lover's eye, she is another Hsi Shi.**   **[C]**

> † Hsi Shi was the famous beauty of ancient China. She was used to debauch the prince of *Wu* and thus cause his defeat.

---

144   Every man sees through his own glasses.   [K]

Western Equivalents

145   Love is blind.

146   Love is not blind; it merely does not see.

147   Beauty is in the eye of the beholder.

148   Love sees no faults.

149   Love makes a good eye squint.

150   Love and reason do not go together.

151   There is one good wife in the country, and every man thinks he has her.

Love: its rules and conditions

152   Love others as you love yourself.   [C]

153   Love others' elders as you love your own.   [C]

154   Love others' youngsters as you love your own.   [C]

155   Love is the love of mankind.   [C]

156   All men are brothers within the Four Seas.   [C]

† "The Four Seas" is synonymous with the English expression of "the Seven Seas."

157   Love extends even to a crow on a roof.   [C]

[144–157]

† The implication of this proverb is that, if you love someone, your love will extend even to things related to your beloved — in this case, your love will extend even to a crow, generally disliked in the Orient, if it should be seen sitting on top of the house of your beloved.

158   **A husband that loves his wife bows down to a post of her parents' home.**   **[K]**

† Synonymous with #157.

159   **Be lovable, and you will be loved.**   **[K]**

160   **Quick to fall in love, quick to get fed up.**   **[J]**

161   **Don't let your passions for another run too wild.** **[J]**

162   **Show your love thin and long.**   **[J]**

† That is, restrain expression of your love to make it last.

163   **Love knows no distinction of birth or station.**   **[J]**

Western Equivalents

164   **Love thy neighbor as thyself.**

165   **Love me, love my dog.**

166   **Praise the child, and you make love to its mother.**

167   **He that loves the tree loves the branch.**

168   **Handsome is as handsome does.**

169   To be loved, be lovable.

170   Hot love, hasty vengeance.

171   Soon hot, soon cold.

172   Love me little, love me long.

173   Love lives in cottages as well as in courts.

Love: its pleasure and pain

174   Love teaches us how capricious life is.   [*J*]

175   It is fortunate to meet a friend, most unfortunate to meet a pretty woman.   [*C*]

176   Love brings constant care and worry.   [*J*]

177   The beginning of love is the end of happiness.   [*J*]

Western Equivalents

178   Love is a sweet torment.

179   Love is sweet in its beginning but sour in its ending.

180   Love is full of busy fear.

181   Love is a bitter weed.

182   War, hunting, and love are as full of trouble as pleasure.

Love and hate

183 Only the truly virtuous man can love or hate others.
[C]

184 We say we hate when we mean we love. [J]

185 Love often breeds anger. [K]

186 Excessive tenderness leads to great hatred. [J]

187 Love is love; fault is fault. [K]

188 Those who possess the same virtue love each other, and those who exercise the same trade hate each other. [C]

189 Who hates a daughter-in-law hates her child, too.
[K]

190 Who hates a priest hates his stole, too. [J]

Western Equivalents

191 Love and hate are blood relations.

192 He that cannot hate cannot love.

193 The greatest hate springs from the greatest love.

194 Love is one-eyed, but hate is blind.

195 Hate is blind as well as love.

196 Love lives a short while, but hate lives long.

[183 — 196]

197 There was never great love that was not followed by great hate.

Parental love

198 The goodness of a father is higher than a mountain; the goodness of a mother is deeper than the sea. [*J*]

199 There are only affectionate fathers and mothers, no affectionate sons and daughters. [*C*]

200 Affection moves downward, but rarely upward. [*K*]

† Synonymous with #199.

201 Buddha's mercy in the parent's mind; unyielding vehemence in the child's mind. [*K*]

202 For the sake of its young the tiger journeys out and back a thousand miles in a single day. [*J*]

203 The lion that wishes its cub to become a lion abandons it in the valley. [*J*]

204 You can never appreciate your parents' love until you have a child of your own. [*J*]

205 Treat the child you love with the rod; treat the child you hate with another cake. [*K*]

206 If you love your son, let him travel on his own. [*J*]

Western Equivalents

207 A mother's love is best of all.

208   A mother's love never ages.

209   No love to a father's.

210   Love is not complete until the grandchild comes.

211   Spare the rod and spoil the child.

212   A whip for a fool, and a rod for a school, is always in good season.

Affection moves downward,
but rarely upward.

213 The best horse needs breaking, and the aptest child needs teaching.

*   *   *

0 what a heaven is love! 0 what a hell!
— *Thomas Dekker*

Love is like war: easy to begin but very hard to stop.
— *H. L. Mencken*

To feed men and not love them is to treat them as if they were barnyard cattle. To love them and not respect them is to treat them as if they were household pets.
— *Mencius*

4 HONESTY

Honesty: its nature

214 Honesty is the most precious jewel.   [K]

215 God dwells in an honest man's mind.   [J]

216   In getting along in the world, be as straight and soft as *tofu*.   [*J*]

   † *Tofu*, or bean cake, is a popular food item in the Orient. It is cut in a cube.

217   Be upright without being punctilious.   [*C*]

218   It is better to be hungry and upright than well fed and unrighteous.   [*C*]

Western Equivalents

219   Be as just as a square and as mild as a lamb.

220   Honesty is the best policy.

221   He is wise that is honest.

222   Plain dealing is a jewel.

223   Let him that would be happy for a day go to the barber; for a week, marry a wife; for a month, buy him a new horse; for a year, build him a new house; for all his lifetime, be an honest man.

A clear conscience: its importance

224   Of all important things, the first is not to cheat conscience.   [*C*]

225   A man with a clear conscience does not fear a knock on the door at midnight.   [*C*]

226   He is truly noble who is free from cares and lives in peace.   [*J*]

227   He who lays aside his conscience for the sake of ambition burns a picture for the sake of its ashes.   [*C*]

228   To act according to one's conscience even behind others' backs.   [*J*]

229   If a man can groom his head every morning, he can also groom his heart every morning.   [*C*]

230   Shave the heart rather than shave the head.   [*J*]

Western Equivalents

231   A good conscience is a soft pillow.

232   A quiet conscience sleeps through thunder.

233   Where there is peace, God is.

234   Open confession is good for the soul.

*   *   *

"Honesty is the best policy," but he who acts on that principle is not an honest man.
— *Richard Whately*

A boy should never be allowed to see an instance of deceit.
— *Confucius*

Consciences differ in different individuals.
— *Abraham Lincoln*

5 COURAGE

Resoluteness: its importance

235 He who is stout-hearted and daring is a man of virtue. [*J*]

236 He that is afraid to shake the dice will never throw a six. [*C*]

237 You can't catch the cubs without entering the tiger's den. [*C*] [*K*] [*J*]

238 If a man has resolution he can live by it; if not, he must live by the toil of his hands. [*C*]

239 Strike against it and be ready to be broken. [*J*]

240 To take a leap with a sword in your teeth. [*K*]

Western Equivalents

241 Courage and resolution are the spirit and soul of virtue.

242 Valor is the nobleness of the mind.

243 Great things are done more through courage than through wisdom.

[235 – 243]

244   **A bold heart is half the battle.**

245   **None but the brave deserve the fair.**

246   **Make your venture, as many a good ship has done.**

False courage or foolhardiness

247   **The newborn pup has no fear of the tiger.**   **[C] [K]**

The newborn pup has no fear of the tiger.

248   **Every dog barks bravely in front of his own door.[J]**

249   **A lion at home, a mouse abroad.**   **[J]**

250   **To swing one's arms while hiding under the bedding.**   **[K]**

Western Equivalents

251   **Every dog is a lion at home.**

252 Every dog is valiant at his own door.

253 Nothing is as bold as a blind mare.

254 He who takes on a lion that is absent fears a mouse that is present.

*　　　*　　　*

Courage stands halfway between cowardice and rashness, one of which is a lack of courage, the other an excess.

— *Plutarch*

When valor preys on reason, it eats the sword it fights with.

— *Shakespeare*

6 PATIENCE

Patience: its rewards

255 Patience is the knot which fastens the seam of victory. [C]

256 Nothing so full of victory as patience. [C]

257 **Patience is a man's lifelong treasure.** [*J*]

258 **With time and patience the mulberry leaf becomes a silk gown.** [*C*]

 † This proverb refers to the long, patient process of silkfarming, in which the silkworm produces raw silk as it feeds on mulberry leaves.

259 **Patience! In time the grass becomes milk.** [*C*]

 † This proverb is synonymous with #258 above. It refers to the long time it takes for the milch cow to produce milk from the grass it feeds on.

260 **Recite "patience" three times, and it will spare you a murder.** [*K*]

261 **Patience in a moment of anger will spare you a hundred days of anguish.** [*C*]

262 **To sit on the bamboo staff for three long years.** [*C*] [*K*]

263 **To sit on the stone for three long years.** [*J*]

264 **Time opens every door to him who waits.** [*C*]

265 **It is easier to die of indignation at the world than it is to live and endure.** [*J*]

Western Equivalents

266 **Patience, time, and money accommodate all things.**

267 **Nature, time, and patience are the three great physicians.**

268 Patience is a plaster for all sores.

269 Patient men win the day.

270 The world is for him who waits.

271 Patience is a remedy for every grief.

Warnings against impatience or anxiety

272 A little impatience will spoil great plans. [C]

273 The first spoonful does not fill your stomach. [K]

274 Ice does not freeze three feet thick with one day's
cold. [C]

275 A frog takes the time to pull back before it jumps. [K]

276 Don't count your badger skins before you have
caught any badgers. [J]

277 To borrow money on a fur while a badger is still in
the den. [K]

278 To set the price of a racoon while it is still in the
den. [J]

279 To try to leap while unable to creep. [K]

280 To buy the saddle before the horse. [J]

281 To get the baby's blanket even before getting a
spouse. [K]

282   Those who swallow their food whole, choke.   [*K*]

Western Equivalents

283   First creep, and then walk.

284   We must learn to walk before we can run.

285   Don't count your chickens before they are hatched.

286   A watched pot never boils.

287   To sit on pins and needles.

288   He who would climb the ladder must begin at the bottom.

289   An oak is not felled at one stroke.

290   Rome was not built in a day.

*   *   *

There is a point when patience ceases to be a virtue.

— *Thomas Morton*

Patience, that blending of moral courage with physical timidity.

— *Thomas Hardy*

7 KNOWLEDGE

Knowledge and learning: their nature and value

291   To accept what one does not know as what one does not know — this is knowledge.   [C]

292   Learning colors a man more than the deepest dye.   [C]

293   Learning is as necessary to a nation as water is to a fish.   [C]

294   Learning is a treasure which accompanies its owner everywhere.   [C]

295   Scholars are a national treasure; wise men are delicacies at the feast.   [C]

Western Equivalents

296   Knowledge is the mother of all virtue; all vice proceeds from ignorance.

297   Knowledge is power.

298   Learning is the eye of the mind.

299   As for me, all I know is that I know nothing.

300   A man's studies pass into his character.

Learning by experience

301   A thousand times heard is not worth one time seen.
[C]

302   Traveling ten thousand miles is better than reading ten thousand books.   [C]

303   It is easier to know how to do a thing than to do it.
[C]

304   One example serves as a criterion for all the rest. [J]

† This proverb assumes that the example in question must have been tested by experience. Proverbs #305 and #306 below are basically synonymous with this proverb.

305   The fall of one leaf heralds the coming of autumn.
[C] [K] [J]

306   To know one is to know ten.   [K]

307   Hunters learn from the birds themselves how to catch them.   [J]

308   To know whether it is long or short, one must actually measure it.   [K]

309   To review old things and learn of new things.
[C] [K] [J]

Traveling ten thousand miles is better than reading ten thousand books.

310   If one wishes to be acquainted with the past and the present, he must read five cartloads of books.   [*C*]

311   To know a man is not to know his face but to know his heart.   [*C*]

312   To know a stream, one must wade through it; to know a man, one must associate with him.   [*K*]

313   The dog near a school will learn to recite lessons in three years.   [*K*]

314   Barrow boys near a temple will learn to chant sutras in no time.   [*J*]

315   The overturned lead cart alerts the carts to the rear.   [*C*]

316   One learns as long as he lives.   [*C*]

Western Equivalents

317   Experience is the best teacher.

318   We learn by doing.

319   He that travels much, knows much.

320   Travel broadens the mind.

321   Example is better than precept.

322   A good example is the best sermon.

323 It is good to learn at other men's cost.

324 Live and learn.

Knowledge with limited vision

325 Ignorance can do you good; knowledge can bring
you trouble.   [K]

326 Learning without wisdom is a load of books on an
ass's back.   [C]

327 The cicada knows nothing of snow.   [C]

328 What does the frog in a well know about the ocean?
[C]

329 A frog in a well.   [K]

   † "A frog in a well" is a sarcastic phrase applied to
   one who knows little about what is going on in the
   outside world.

330 A frog in a well is ignorant of the vast sea.   [J]

331 To observe the sky from within a well.   [C] [K]

332 To the frog in a well, heaven is only a sieve in size.
[C]

333 To look into the sky through a needle's eye. [C] [K]

334 A man standing behind the wall can see only the
wall.   [K]

335 The foot of the lamp is the worst lighted.   [C] [K]

336 It is darkest about the candleholder's feet. [*J*]

337 The eyes do not see the eyelashes. [*C*]

Western Equivalents

338 Knowledge is folly, except grace guide it.

339 A little learning is a dangerous thing.

340 Learning in the breast of a bad man is as a sword in the hand of a madman.

341 Much science, much sorrow.

342 He that stays in the valley shall never get over the hill.

343 Know thyself.

344 Much water runs by the mill that the miller knows not of.

345 To see no farther than the end of one's nose.

Unfortunate experience: its effects

346 A heart once frightened by a turtle dreads the lid of a pot. [*C*] [*K*]

347 A man scalded by hot soup blows at a bowl of cold water. [*K*]

348 He that has been scalded by hot soup blows at a cold fish salad. [*J*]

349 A man once bitten by a snake fears a rotted rope. [*J*]

350 An ox that has had sunstroke pants at sight of the moon.   [*C*] [*K*]

Western Equivalents

351 A burnt child dreads the fire.

352 A scalded cat fears cold water.

353 He that has been bitten by a serpent is afraid of a rope.

354 Birds once snared fear all bushes.

355 Once bitten, twice shy.

*   *   *

"Know thyself?" If I knew myself, I'd run away.
— *Goethe*

To know and yet think we do not know is the highest attainment; not to know and yet think we do know is a disease.
— *Lao-tzu*

Thinking without learning makes one flighty, and learning without thinking is a disaster.
— *Confucius*

The love of money and the love of learning rarely meet.
— *George Herbert*

8 WISDOM

Wisdom: its nature and worth

356 Wisdom is the knowledge possessed by all mankind. [C]

357 Wisdom and virtue are like the wheels of a cart. [J]

358 Wealth is a treasure for a lifetime, wisdom a treasure for all time. [J]

359 Learning without wisdom is a load of books on an ass's back. [J]

360 A wise man is not a mere tool for a single purpose, but is versatile in every field. [C] [J]

Western Equivalents

361 Without wisdom, wealth is worthless.

362 Wit and wisdom are eternally precious.

363 You may be a wise man though you cannot make a watch.

364 Wisdom is better than strength.

Prudence: an element of wisdom

365 The wise man never gets close to danger. [*J*]

366 He who rouses a sleeping tiger exposes himself to danger. [*C*]

367 To poke the nose of a sleeping tiger. [*K*]

368 A hole in the ice is dangerous only to those who go skating. [*C*]

369 In a melon field adjust not thy sandals; under a plum tree arrange not thy hat. [*C*] [*K*]

† Adjusting the sandals or arranging the hat may make it appear you are up to something. This caution is given so that one may not be suspected of stealing.

370 Forethought is easy; repentance is hard. [*C*]

371 Those who do not give any forethought to their future will find trouble at their doorstep. [*C*] [*J*]

372 The wise man does not treat those who are already sick but those who are not yet ill. [*C*] [*J*]

373 Even if the stream is shallow, wade it as if it were deep. [*K*] [*J*]

374 You cannot prevent the buds of sadness from flying over your head, but you can prevent them from nesting in your hair. [*C*]

Western Equivalents

375 What is not wisdom is danger.

*He who rouses a sleeping tiger
exposes himself to danger.*

376   Let sleeping dogs lie.

377   Wake not a sleeping lion.

378   Forewarned is forearmed.

379   He that looks not before finds himself behind.

380   No safe wading in unknown water.

[376—380]

381   Prevention is better than cure.

Other signs of wisdom

382   Wise is the man who has two loaves, and sells one
       to buy a lily.   [C]

383   A wise man does not blame fools.   [J]

384   To admit what one does not know is a sign of
       wisdom.   [J]

385   Enlightened men pronounce sentence on themselves.
                                                         [C]

386   Wise men care not for what they cannot have.   [C]

387   The wise man is great in small things; the petty
       man is small in great things.   [C]

388   The wise man doesn't tell what he does, and never
       does what cannot be told.   [C]

389   He is wise who avoids quarrels.   [C]

390   The wise can adapt themselves to any change in
       circumstances.   [C] [J]

391   There is one phoenix to be found in every thousand
       chickens.   [K]

       † The phoenix is considered a more spiritually en-
       dowed bird than the chicken. The implication of this
       proverb is that wise men are very hard to find in this
       world.

392 **Even Confucius was ignored in his own time.** [C] [J]

   † The implication of this proverb is that being popular in his own time is not the criterion of a wise man.

Western Equivalents

393 **The most manifest sign of wisdom is a continual cheerfulness.**

394 **It is a great point of wisdom to find out one's own folly.**

395 **Fools bite one another, but wise men agree together.**

396 **A wise man changes his mind, a fool never.**

397 **He that is truly wise and great, lives both too early and too late.**

Wisdom through experience

398 **To become useful jade must be carved; to become wise a man must experience adversity.** [C]

399 **The older a man is, the wiser he becomes; the older a thing is, the uglier it becomes.** [K]

400 **Difficulties make jewels out of men.** [J]

401 **An old stager that fought all sorts of battles in life.** [K]

   † This proverb reads literally: "He has been in all the mountain-battles and sea-battles."

Western Equivalents

402   No man is born wise or learned.

403   Experience is the mother of wisdom.

404   The wind in one's face makes one wise.

405   Adversity makes a man wise, not rich.

406   Trouble brings experience and experience brings
       wisdom.

The wise man and the fool

407   The greatest wisdom seems like foolishness.   [C]

408   A wise man at times pretends to be a fool.   [J]

409   He who knows he is a fool is not a big fool.   [C]

410   First comes foolishness and last comes wisdom.   [K]

411   Clever men are often employed by fools.   [C]

412   After-counsel is a fool's counsel.   [J]

413   Rumors stop when they are heard by wise men;
       fools keep them going.   [J]

414   The wise never speak ill even of those with whom
       they have severed relations.   [J]

Western Equivalents

415   A wise man may sometimes play the fool.

416   No man can play the fool so well as the wise man.

417   What the fool does in the end, the wise man does at the start.

418   Fools are wise after the event.

419   Easy to be wise after the event.

420   A fool may give a wise man counsel.

421   Wise men have their mouths in their hearts, and fools their hearts in their mouths.

*   *   *

You look wise. Pray correct that error.
— *Charles Lamb*

Few are those who err on the side of self-restraint.
— *Confucius*

The wise man reads both books and life itself.
— *Lin Yutang*

All human wisdom is summed up in two words — wait and hope.
— *Alexandre Dumas*

CHAPTER TWO

The Vices

"THE SINFUL, immoral nature of man," — so declared many of the world's theologians and moral philosophers. The very same negative qualities in men — qualities contrary to good morals and proper ways of living — have been observed over and over by diverse groups of people in many nations and cultures. The list of the vices in this section is far from complete; it focuses on those traits that have attracted considerable attention in China, Korea, and Japan through many generations. Curiously enough, these three Asian nations showed in their proverbs less concern than their Western counterparts with such traits as lust, gluttony, hypocrisy, and sloth.

1 ANGER

Anger: its effects

422   When a man is angry, he cannot be in the right. [C]

423   When wrath speaks, wisdom veils her face.   [C]

424   In a fit of anger a woman cuckolds her husband. [K]

425   Laughter cannot recall what anger has banished. [J]

426   To get slapped on the cheek on Chongno and scowl at the Han River.   [K]

    † Chongno is a main street in downtown Seoul and the Han River is about ten miles away. This proverb and the three proverbs which follow caution against people's tendency to transfer their anger from the cause to another object.

427   To get slapped on the cheek at a mountain park and beat the woman back at home.   [K]

428   To get beaten in a wrestling match and beat the wife back at home.   [J]

429   To avenge oneself in Nagasaki for a wrong received in Edo.   [J]

† Nagasaki is a city at the western end of Japan, and Edo, the capital city during the Edo Era, was situated where today's Tokyo is.

430 **A man kicks a stone from anger only to hurt his own toe.** [K]

431 **An angry man kicking a stone.** [C] [K]

† A familiar image describing one of the commonest actions of an angry man.

Western Equivalents

432 **When a man gets angry, his reason rides out.**

433 **Anger begins with folly and ends with repentance.**

434 **He that is angry is seldom at ease.**

435 **An angry man never wants woe.**

436 **Many a man blames his wife for his own thriftlessness.**

Warnings and remedies against anger

437 **Regard anger as your enemy.** [J]

438 **If a teacup is thrown at you, receive it with a cotton napkin.** [J]

439 **The more quick-tempered you are, the more likely you will become a pauper.** [J]

440 **Die of anger, but don't go to the law.** [C]

441 Patience in a moment of anger will spare you a
hundred days of anguish. [C]

442 Recite "patience" three times, and it will spare you
a murder. [K]

443 When angry, think of the love of your parents for
you. [J]

Western Equivalents

444 Anger is a short madness.

445 When you enter a house, leave your anger ever at
the door.

446 When angry, count ten before you speak; if very
angry, a hundred.

447 A soft answer turneth away wrath.

448 Two things a man should never be angry at: what
he can help, and what he cannot help.

*   *   *

Anyone can become angry — that is easy, but to be
angry with the right person, to the right degree, at
the right time, for the right purpose, and in the
right way — this is not easy.

— *Aristotle*

Touch me with noble anger.

— *Shakespeare*

2 ENVY AND JEALOUSY

Envy as universal malady

449 Envy is one's own enemy.   [*J*]

450 The devil peers enviously into a house of means. [*J*]

451 My cousin has bought a farm, and I have heartburn.
                                                              [*K*]

452 My neighbor has had a storehouse built, and I have
     heartburn.   [*J*]

453 To put ash into the forbidden bowl of rice.   [*K*]

454 To puncture the forbidden persimmon.   [*K*]

455 Those who possess the same virtue love each other,
     and those who exercise the same trade hate each
     other.   [*C*]

Western Equivalents

456 Riches bring care and envy.

457 Envy eats nothing but its own heart.

458 Envy shoots at others, but wounds herself.

To puncture the forbidden persimmon.

459   The envious man shall never want woe.

460   I am Envy. I cannot read, and therefore wish all books were burnt.

461   One potter envies another.

Jealousy and love

462   Jealousy is the soul of love.   [*J*]

463   Nine women out of ten are jealous.   [*C*]

464 One wishes his servant weren't a big eater and his wife weren't all jealousy. [K]

Western Equivalents

465 Love is never without jealousy.

466 Love, being jealous, makes a good eye asquint.

467 Love and lordship like no fellowship.

*   *   *

Whoever envies another confesses his superiority.
— *Samuel Johnson*

Every other sin hath some pleasure annexed to it, or will admit of an excuse: envy alone wants both.
— *Robert Burton*

3 GREED

Greed: its nature and effects

468 Avarice goes before destruction. [K] [J]

469 Avarice is like snow: the higher it piles up, the more it clouds your path. [J]

470   A sea can be filled, a covetous man's wants never.
[K]

471   The covetous hawk can't feel his talons ripping off.
[J]

472   Get him a horse to ride, and he will want a groom as well.   [K]

473   Greed's tub is bottomless.   [J]

474   The crane envies the turtle his long life.   [J]

† The crane's long life is also well known in the Far East.

475   The more you achieve, the more you will crave. [C]

476   To reckon the small but ignore the large.   [C] [K]

477   To grudge one dollar and lose a hundred.   [J]

478   If you run after the other running hare, you will lose the one in hand.   [K]

479   Run after both the horsefly and the bee, and you will catch neither.   [J]

Western Equivalents

480   Covetousness is the root of all evil.

481   Poverty wants many things, but covetousness all.

482   Avarice is the only passion that never ages.

[470 − 482]

To grudge one dollar and lose a hundred.

483   Give him an inch and he will take a yard.

484   Beggars' bags are bottomless.

485   The more you get, the more you want.

486   Penny-wise and pound-foolish.

487   If you run after two hares at once, you will catch
       neither.

488   Grasp all, lose all.

[483 — 488]

Remedies against covetousness

489 Do not fall into avarice if you want to gather up
riches. [*J*]

490 Ninety-percent attainment of your desire is the best
you can wish for. [*J*]

491 He who does not covet and can control his words
will be comfortable wherever he goes. [*C*]

Western Equivalents

492 Covet all, lose all.

493 The pleasure of what we enjoy is lost by coveting
more.

494 Don't have too many irons in the fire.

495 Kill not the goose that lays the golden egg.

† A proverb based on a fable. According to this fable, a greedy owner of a goose which laid a golden
egg every day killed the bird in the vain hope of
finding a store of gold inside it.

*   *   *

No wealth can satisfy the covetous desire of wealth.
— *Jeremy Taylor*

Though ye take from a covetous man all his treasure, he has yet one jewel left; ye cannot bereave
him of his covetousness.
— *John Milton*

4 SELFISHNESS

Self-centeredness as man's nature

496 There is no elbow that bends outward.   [C] [K]

   † Every man's interest is directed toward himself before others.

497 The autumn cloud is thin, but man's goodwill is thinner.   [C]

498 Just so long as you ask nothing, man's nature is bland.   [C]

499 He knows the value of the seven pennies in his own purse, but hardly knows the value of the fourteen pennies in others'.   [K]

500 Nothing to help the poor with, we say, but there's always something to be stolen from our home.   [K]

501 The old raven laughs at the blackness of the pig and knows nothing of his own ugliness.   [J]

502 To draw water to serve one's own rice field only.
    [C] [K]

503   **To wrestle with another using his loincloth.**   **[*J*]**

> † A Japanese wrestler usually wears a loincloth dur-
> ing the game. This proverb cautions against man's
> tendency to utilize someone else's resources to achieve
> his selfish goal.

504   **We can bear others' pains even for three years.** **[*J*]**

Western Equivalents

505   **Every man is nearest himself.**

506   **The parson always christens his own child first.**

507   **Some men go through a forest and see no firewood.**

508   **Injuries we write in marble, kindness in dust.**

509   **The raven chides blackness.**

510   **The burden is light on the shoulder of another.**

511   **It is easier to bear the misfortune of others.**

Ingratitude: an element of selfishness

512   **To drink water and forget him who dug the well.** **[*C*]**

513   **To dismantle the bridge after crossing the river.** **[*C*]**

514   **To be bitten by one's own dog.** **[*K*]**

515   **To be chopped on the foot by one's own trusty axe.**
   [*K*]

516   To enjoy the shade of a tree and break off its branch.
                                                          [C]

517   A man who has eaten a whole horse complains it
      had horsy smell.   [K]

518   A man who has eaten his fill says it had beefy smell.
                                                          [J]

519   Those admitted free grumble most about the play.
                                                          [C]

520   Save a traveler from drowning, and he'll turn and
      demand his baggage.   [K]

Western Equivalents

521   Gratitude is the least of virtues, ingratitude the worst
      of vices.

522   To be stabbed in the back.

523   To bite the hand that feeds you.

524′ The hog never looks up to him that threshes down
      the acorns.

Self-love: a beneficial quality

525   Yourself first, others afterward.   [C]

526   Heaven will not betray anyone who is devoted to his
      purpose.   [C]

527   Love others as you love yourself.   [C]

Western Equivalents

528   Self-preservation is the first law of nature.

529   Every man for himself, and God for us all.

530   Mind other men, but most yourself.

531   Near is my shirt, nearer is my skin.

532   Love thy neighbor as thyself.

*   *   *

Selfishness is not living as one wishes to live. It is asking others to live as one wishes to live.
— *Oscar Wilde*

Self-love, as it happens to be well or ill conducted, constitutes virtue and vice.
— *La Rochefoucauld*

5 PRIDE

Pride and self-praise: their dangers

533   A proud man is sure to fall.   [*K*]

534   Pride means the end of wisdom.   [*J*]

535   The conceited man stinks.   [C]

536   The proud Heike clan, the cause of its downfall. [J]

     † The Heike clan in old Japan once boasted of its pomp and splendor as the Roman Empire did in the West.

537   Self-praise ends in a disastrous fire.   [K]

Western Equivalents

538   Pride goeth before destruction, and a haughty spirit before a fall.

539   Pride is a flower that grows in the devil's garden.

540   Pride increases our enemies, but puts our friends to flight.

541   A man's praise in his own mouth stinks.

The proud: their characteristics

542   A proud gentleman wouldn't attempt the dog paddle even though he were to drown.   [K]

543   The fashionable would rather catch cold than put on more clothes.   [J]

544   When a daughter-in-law grows into a mother-in-law, she ends up being haughtier.   [K]

545   The proud frog forgets when he was a tadpole. [K]

Western Equivalents

546   There are those who despise with a greater pride.

547   Pride had rather go out of the way than go behind.

548   Pride will spit in pride's face.

549   It is a proud horse that will not bear his own provender.

Boasting and exaggeration

550   Every melon seller praises his own melons.   [C]

551   The quack doctor likes to talk of his own medical feats.   [J]

552   A total fool boasts of his wife, a half fool of his children.   [C] [K]

553   Those who praise themselves are in the company of fools.   [J]

554   Empty carriages make a louder noise.   [K]

555   To make a big staff out of a small needle.   [C] [K] [J]

Western Equivalents

556   A vaunter and a liar are near akin.

557   He that praises himself spatters himself.

558   They can do least who boast loudest.

559 Great braggers, little doers.

560 Empty vessels make the greatest sound.

561 To make a mountain out of a molehill.

Pride and humility

562 Pride beckons disasters; humility invites reward. [C]

563 An egg should never argue with a rock. [C]

564 He who would stand up in the world must first learn to stoop. [C]

565 A wise student questions his own skill, not his examiner's competence. [C]

566 The riper the grain is, the lower it hangs its head. [K] [J]

567 Never be boastful; someone may pass who knew you as a child. [C]

568 Humbleness may often be counted among acts of pride. [J]

Western Equivalents

569 He that will not stoop for a pin shall never be worth a pound.

570 Remember you are but a man.

571 No man is indispensable.

*The riper the grain is,
the lower it hangs its head.*

572   The best of men are but men at best.

573   Pride often wears the cloak of humility.

*   *   *

Likeness begets love, yet proud men hate one another.

— *Thomas Fuller*

Pride does not wish to owe and vanity does not wish to pay.

— *La Rochefoucauld*

6 CRITICISM AND SLANDER

Blaming others: its nature and effects

574   However stupid a man may be, he grows clever enough when blaming others; however wise, he becomes a dolt when blaming himself.   [C]

575   People criticizing what they cannot understand are like blind men fumbling with an elephant.   [J]

576   The withered broad leaf complains the pine needle rustles too loud.   [K]

577 The dog dirtied with manure reproves the dog covered with bran dust. [*K*]

578 The unripe persimmon condoles the ripe persimmon. [*J*]

† The unripe fruit expresses sympathy because it thinks that the ripe persimmon has lost its youthful color.

579 A bad calligrapher is choosy about his brushes. [*J*]

580 The offspring always blames his ancestors for his own failures. [*K*]

581 The blind man blames the ditch for his fall. [*K*]

Western Equivalents

582 You can see a mole in another's eye but cannot see a bean in your own.

583 The eye that sees all things else sees not itself.

584 The pot calls the kettle black.

585 The kettle calls the pot burnt ass.

586 A bad workman always blames his tools.

587 The hunchback does not see his own hump, but sees his companion's.

Remedies against criticism and slander

588 Heaven's virtue is "to let live." [*C*]

[577–588]

589　Let others take their own way, and I take my own.
　　　　　　　　　　　　　　　　　　　　　[J]

590　Do not pass comment on the frost on your neighbor's roof while there is still snow in your own doorway. [C]

591　If you do not discuss the faults of others, no one will blame you for not discussing your own.　　　[C]

592　When one falls, it is not the foot that is to blame.[C]

593　Whoever suffered for not speaking ill of others? [C]

594　Blame yourself as you would blame others; excuse others as you would excuse yourself.　　　　　[C]

595　Before you blame others for one thing, think of your own ten faults.　　　　　　　　　　　　　　[K]

596　A wise student questions his own skill, not his examiner's competence.　　　　　　　　　　　[C]

597　Deal with the faults of others as gently as you do your own.　　　　　　　　　　　　　　　　[C]

598　Do not let slander enter in by the ears and go down to the heart.　　　　　　　　　　　　　　　[C]

599　Slander cannot injure the upright, for when the water recedes the stone is still there.　　　　[C]

Western Equivalents

600　Live and let live.

601   Those who live in glass houses should not throw
       stones.

602   He that flings dirt at another dirtieth himself most.

603   Slander flings stones at itself.

604   The remedy for injuries, is not to remember them.

*   *   *

Be thou as chaste as ice, as pure as snow, thou
shalt not escape calumny.
                                    — Shakespeare

Truth is generally the best vindication against slander.
                                    — Abraham Lincoln

A man's faults all conform to his type of mind.
Observe his faults and you may know his virtues.
                                    — Confucius

CHAPTER THREE

The Ineffectual

A MAN'S life is, by and large, a series of attempts to accomplish what one has in mind. In this sense, life may be summed up as a series of successes and failures. Failure is just as common as success in any man's life. As illustrated in this section, a great deal of failings come from man's lack of good sense and judgment. Because these failings are terribly out of place, they do provide a funny side to life. Closely related to this comic vision of man is a view that man is by nature liable to err.

1 FOOLISHNESS

Foolishness: lack of sense and judgment

605   When the light of new day shows in the east, a fool takes it for the best possible world.   [C] [K]

606   When it is bright, a fool takes it for a moonlit night. [J]

607   The foolish pheasant buries his head in the grass and thinks he is not seen.   [K]

608   To hide the head and leave the rear-end uncovered. [J]

609   To fill with a spade what should have been filled with a hoe.   [K]

610   To climb a tree to catch a fish.   [C] [K] [J]

611   To ascend a mountain to catch fish.   [K]

612   To spare a tile and spoil the beams of the house. [C] [K]

613   To kill the ox while straightening its horns.   [J]

[605 — 613]

614 **To spill the sesame oil and start scrambling for sesame seeds.** [K]

† A great deal of time and energy needs to be expended to get sesame oil from sesame seeds. Thus, it is foolish to spill the oil carelessly and start gathering sesame seeds all over again.

615 **Let one blind man lead another and both will fall in the river.** [C]

616 **The fool in a hurry drinks his tea with chopsticks.** [C]

To ascend a mountain to catch fish.

Western Equivalents

617 Bright rain makes fools fain.

618 The foolish ostrich buries his head in the sand and thinks he is not seen.

619 He is a fool that makes a hammer of his fist.

620 If the blind lead the blind, both shall fall into the ditch.

621 It is a foolish sheep that makes the wolf his confessor.

622 It is a blind goose that comes to the fox's sermon.

Foolishness: futile endeavors

623 A blunt knife may be honed on a whetstone, but if a man is stupid there is no honing his wit. [C]

624 Whom Heaven at his birth has endowed as a fool, 'tis a waste of instruction to teach. [C]

625 There's no help for the poor even with all the money in the treasury. [K]

626 No medicine to cure a fool. [J]

627 A fool is a fool until the day he dies. [J]

628 Being content with only a kind word is ineffectual as a dragon-fly sipping water. [C]

629 Do not seek to escape a flood by clutching a tiger's tail.   [C]

630 Kindness shown to a starfish is like a gust of wind in the desert.   [C]

631 A fog cannot be dispelled with a fan.   [J]

632 A blind man's mirror and a monk's comb.   [J]

† A blind man has no need for a mirror and a Buddhist monk has no need for a comb.

633 Laughter cannot bring back what anger has driven away.   [J]

634 To draw a picture of a cake to satisfy hunger.
                                                  [C] [K]

635 To get dressed in brocade and stroll in the dark.
                                              [C] [K] [J]

† The implication here is that even though one has had great success in life, it is futile when that success is not duly recognized by the right kind of people.

636 To make an offering to an undesignated temple. [K]

637 The east wind to a horse's ear.   [C] [K] [J]

† The notoriously insensitive horse pays little attention to the agreeable spring wind. The following two proverbs are synonymous with this proverb.

638 To read sutra to the ears of an ox.   [C] [K] [J]

639 To give a gold coin to a cat.   [J]

640 **It's like talking to the stone wall.** [*K*]

† This is said of a futile attempt to persuade a stupid and silly person.

641 **It's like ants trying to move a colossal statue of Buddha.** [*J*]

642 **To preach a sermon to Buddha.** [*K*]

643 **To teach sutra to Buddha.** [*J*]

644 **To look for a needle on the sea-bed.** [*C*]

645 **To look for a needle in the grass.** [*K*]

To preach a sermon to Buddha.

646 To measure the vault of heaven with a bamboo pole. [*K*]

647 To strike at the stars with a bamboo pole. [*J*]

648 It's useless to make an image of Buddha without putting a soul in. [*J*]

649 To build a mansion in the air. [*C*] [*K*]

650 To build a castle with eggs. [*K*]

651 To chase from land the boat thief sailing away. [*J*]

652 To try to fill in a well with snow. [*C*]

653 To try to fill in a pond with salt. [*J*]

654 As useless as pouring water on the sand. [*K*]

655 To try to fill a bottomless jar with water. [*K*]

656 An awl that's lost its point is of little use. [*K*]

Western Equivalents

657 He that is born a fool is never cured.

658 Send a fool to the market and a fool he will return again.

659 Send a donkey to Paris, and he will return no wiser than he went.

660 A forced kindness deserves no thanks.

661   Swine, women, and bees cannot be turned.

662   Do not cast your pearls before swine.

663   Talking to the wall.

664   Don't teach your grandmother to suck eggs.

665   To teach a fish how to swim.

666   To teach a dog to chase rabbits.

667   To teach the Pope how to pray.

668   You can't teach an old dog new tricks.

669   To build castles in the air.

*   *   *

If others had not been foolish, we should be so.
— *William Blake*

He who lives free from folly is not so wise as he thinks.
— *La Rochefoucauld*

2 INCONGRUITY

Incongruity: lack of correspondence

670 To make a big staff out of a small needle. [C] [K] [J]

671 To blast a sparrow with a cannon.   [C]

672 To burn one's house to chase the bedbugs away. [K]

673 What begins as a dragon's head often ends in a
snake's tail.   [C]

674 To paint chrysanthemums on straw shoes.   [K]

† According to Korean tradition, colorful chrysanthemums were painted on the silk shoes of women of
well-to-do families, while straw shoes were worn by
women of low-income families.

675 To decorate the pigsty with a bronze lock.   [K]

676 A brass horseshoe on a dog's paw.   [K]

677 Like oil floating on cold water.   [K]

678 Oil and water do not mix.   [J]

679 A farmer plowing the field in formal attire.   [K]

680   His belly button is bigger than his belly.   [K]

681   The thread is thicker than its needle.   [K]

682   While one talks of a marriage, another talks of a funeral.   [K]

683   To trim the foot to fit the shoe.   [C]

Western Equivalents

684   To make a mountain out of a molehill.

685   To make an elephant out of a fly.

686   Never use a rock to break an egg when you can do it with the back of your knife.

687   Take not a musket to kill a butterfly.

688   Burn not your house to fright the mouse away.

689   To start off with a bang and to end with a whimper.

Warnings against incongruity

690   To be neither high nor low is as much as a man could want.   [C]

691   To go beyond is as bad as to fall short.   [C]

692   Too much is no better than too little.   [J]

693   If a wren tries to walk like a stork, he will break his crotch.   [K]

694 Make your hat according to the size of your head.
[C]

695 A pine caterpiller must eat the pine needles, nothing
else.   [K]

696 Crabs dig holes to fit their shells.   [J]

697 First see how much space you have, then stretch
your legs.   [K]

698 Consult your purse before you buy.   [J]

Western Equivalents

699 Too much of ought is good for nought.

700 In excess, even nectar is poison.

701 Too far east is west.

702 Mirth without measure is madness.

703 Don't bite off more than you can chew.

704 Cut your coat according to the cloth.

705 Stretch your arm no farther than your sleeve will
reach.

706 Stretch your legs according to your coverlet.

*   *   *

Laughter almost ever cometh of things most dis-
proportioned to ourselves, and nature.
— *Philip Sidney*

Impropriety is the soul of wit.
— *W. Somerset Maugham*

3 IMPERFECTION

Fallibility: its nature and effects

707 Even the immortals sometimes drop their swords.
[C]

708 Even the tiger sometimes falls into a doze.   [C]

709 Even a monkey sometimes fall from a tree.   [K] [J]

710 Even an old cat may get its whiskers burnt.   [C]

711 Even Kōbō's brush slipped from time to time.   [J]

† Kōbō was a great calligrapher in old Japan.

712 Being a human being, who has no fault?   [C]

[707—712]

713 How often does a man's teeth bite his own tongue ? [*J*]

714 There's nobody you can shake off without stirring up some dust. [*K*]

715 Even jade can have a flaw. [*K*]

716 There's no dipper which never bumps the cooking pot. [*C*]

717 There are cracked pots and mended lids anywhere you look. [*K*]

718 Some lids fit their vessel and some don't. [*J*]

719 Do not bear grievances, always forgive whenever possible. [*C*]

Some lids fit their vessel and some don't.

Western Equivalents

720 Even Homer sometimes nods.

721 No man is infallible.

722 Every man has his faults.

723 Every bean has its black.

724 No garden without its weeds.

725 No rose without a thorn.

726 Every one has a skeleton in his closet.

727 Every shoe fits not every foot.

728 To err is human; to forgive divine.

Faultiness: its effects vis-a-vis the specialist

729 The son of a great doctor usually dies of disease. [C]

730 A fortune teller cannot read his own fortune.   [K]

731 A physician cannot heal himself.   [K] [J]

732 A monk cannot cut his own hair.   [K]

733 An axe cannot chop its own handle.   [K]

734 A palanquin carrier never rides in a palanquin.   [C]

735 No knife to be found in the blacksmith's kitchen. [K]

[720 − 735]

736 A seamstress that makes three undershirts a night can't afford one for herself. [*K*]

737 Those raised on the river will drown in the river. [*C*]

738 Great swimmers die in the water, good riders at shooting. [*J*]

Western Equivalents

739 The shoemaker's son always goes barefoot.

740 None worse shod than the shoemaker's wife and the smith's mare.

741 Physician, heal thyself.

742 Accidents will happen in the best-regulated families.

743 Wise men are caught in wiles.

*   *   *

All things are literally better, lovelier, and more beloved for the imperfections which have been divinely appointed, that the law of human life may be effort, and the law of human judgment mercy.
— *John Ruskin*

It is well that there is no one without a fault, for he would not have a friend in the world.
— *Wenworth Dillon*

Chapter Four

Senses and Sensibilities

AS ITS title implies, this section is concerned with man's capacity for feeling and perceiving. Here, the power of the human mind responds at one level to such bodily stimuli as the eyes, ears, and nerves; at another level the power of feeling involves awareness of something emotional, or even elemental, in life. In either case, however, we note that men of the past never failed to ponder and pursue the enduring value of humble desires in the human heart. Worthy of special attention are those proverbs listed under "Silence: its value," "Feminine beauty: its shallowness," "Feminine beauty: its ill-fatedness and dangers," "Happiness. its nature and sources," and "Happiness: its secrets."

1 SPEECH

Words: their nature and value

744 Words are sounds of the heart.   [C]

745 One kind word will keep you warm for three
winters.   [C] [J]

746 For one word a man is often deemed wise; for one
word a man is often deemed foolish.   [C]

747 The gift of a good word may settle a thousand-dollar
debt.   [K]

748 One word can be worth a thousand pieces of gold.
[C] [K]

749 It's more in how you say it than what you say.   [K]

750 A gentle word brings a gentle answer.   [K]

751 The more you chew your meat, the better it tastes;
the more you speak, the lighter your heart becomes.
[K]

752 To refrain from saying what you have to say makes
you sulky.   [J]

753 **Speak straight even if your mouth is crooked.** **[K]**

> † The implication is that it is important to be direct and candid when you speak. The clause, "your mouth is crooked," may be taken as a rhetorical device against the clause, "speak straight."

754 **The baby that cries gets the milk.** **[K]**

Western Equivalents

755 **The tongue is the rudder of our ship.**

756 **The bird is known by his note, the man by his words.**

757 **He that speaks well fights well.**

758 **A kind word is like a spring day.**

759 **Good words cost nothing, but are worth much.**

760 **Changing of words is the lightening of hearts.**

761 **The lame tongue gets nothing.**

762 **The squeaking wheel gets the grease.**

The tongue: its dangers

763 **The mouth is the front gate to all misfortune.** **[J]**

764 **You can recover an arrow that has been shot, but not a word that has been said.** **[K]**

[753 — 764]

765 Once a word is let out, the swiftest horse cannot overtake it. [C]

766 Four strong horses cannot overtake one spoken word. [J]

767 The more one talks, the more he blunders. [C]

768 The more you talk, the greater your chance of a slip of the tongue. [K]

769 When words are many, there must be error. [C]

770 The more you grind your grain, the finer it becomes; the more you speak, the coarser your relations with others become. [K]

771 Words are often made angular by the way they are said. [J]

772 Harsh words bring harsh words in return. [J]

773 Wounds inflicted by a sword may heal; wounds afflicted by words will fester. [J]

774 The tongue of a woman is a sword that never rusts. [J]

Western Equivalents

775 The tongue talks at the head's cost.

776 Words have wings, and cannot be recalled.

777 A word and a stone let go cannot be called back.

778 Talk much, err much.

779 Better the foot slip than the tongue.

780 One ill word asks another.

781 The tongue is more venomous than a serpent's sting.

782 Words cut sharper than swords.

Silence: its value

783 Silence is of the gods; monkeys chatter. [C]

784 Silence is the sweet medicine of the heart. [C]

785 Few troubles, few dreams; few words, few faults. [C]

786 He who expands his heart contracts his mouth. [C]

787 Those who know much talk little; those who know little talk much. [C]

788 What goes unsaid is a flower. [J]

† It is better to leave something unsaid than to have it spoken out.

789 Leave your talk unsaid; leave your dish unconsumed. [J]

790 The bottle filled with water makes no sound when it is shaken. [C] [K]

791 Stop up your mouth like a bottle neck; guard your thoughts like a fort. [C]

792 A good listener is better than a good talker. [C]

793 A wise man has long ears and a short tongue. [J]

794 The silent man is often worth listening to. [J]

795 Breathe out as you will, speak out as you dare. [K]

796 It is beneficial to keep both your purse and your mouth shut. [J]

797 Save what you want to say today till tomorrow. [J]

798 Words must not be spoken foolishly; what you say must accord with reason. [C]

Western Equivalents

799 Speech is silver; silence is golden.

800 Wise men keep silent, fools talk.

801 Few words are best.

802 He who enlarges his heart restricts his tongue.

803 He knows most who speaks least.

804 A wise head makes a closed mouth.

805 Half a word is enough for a wise man.

806 Listen much, speak little.

807   Keep your mouth shut and your ears open.

808   Tell not all you know, all you have, or all you can do.

Keep your mouth shut and your ears open.

Idle talk: its nature and effects

809   Whispered words are heard afar.   [*C*]

810   What is told in a man's ear is often heard a hundred
       miles away.   [*C*]

811   Even the footless word will travel a thousand miles.
                                                           [*K*]

812   Pass round words, and they will pile up; pass round
       cakes, and they will diminish.   [*K*]

813   Gossiping is as easy as eating cold gruel.   [*C*] [*K*]

814   Gossip lasts but seventy-five days.   [*J*]

       † A reference that any idle talk about other people
       and their affairs does not prevail long — a couple of
       months or so at the most.

815   Gossip dies down in three months.   [*K*]

       ### *Western Equivalents*

816   Bad news travels fast.

817   Ill news comes apace.

818   Go abroad and you'll hear of home.

819   A wonder lasts but nine days.

Warnings against idle talk

820   Partitions have chinks, and walls have ears.   [*C*]

821   Walls have ears, and doors have eyes.   [*C*]

822   Sparrows hear you talk in the day, and mice hear
      you talk in the night.   [*C*] [*K*]

823   If you converse on the road, remember there may
      be men in the grass.   [*C*]

824   Speak of Ts'ao Ts'ao, and he is sure to appear.   [*C*]

      † A forerunner in founding the state of *Wei* during
      the period of the Three Kingdoms in China, Ts'ao
      Ts'ao was known to be very crafty and clever.

825   Speak of the tiger, and it surely will show up.   [*K*]

826   Start gossiping about someone, and just as soon his
      shadow will show up.   [*J*]

   Western Equivalents

827   Walls have ears.

828   Fields have eyes, and woods have ears.

829   Speak of the devil, and he is sure to appear.

830   Speak of the wolf, and you will see its tail come up.

831   Talk of the donkey, and it will come trotting up.

Rumor: its plausibility and implausibility

832   There is no smoke without fire.   [*C*] [*J*]

833   Will there be smoke where there is no fire?   [*K*]

834 Does the drum sound when it is not beaten? [K]

835 Spread a rumor, and someone else's lie will become your lie. [J]

Western Equivalents

836 Where there's smoke, there's a fire.

837 Where there are reeds, there is water.

838 Where there is whispering, there is lying.

839 Gossiping and lying go together.

Words and deeds

840 Words are mere bubbles of water, but deeds are drops of gold. [C]

841 There are far fewer men of deeds than men of words. [K]

842 It is easy to say but hard to do. [J]

843 The empty carriage makes the louder noise. [K]

844 An empty cask makes a loud noise. [J]

Western Equivalents

845 Deeds are fruits; words are but leaves.

846 Good words without deeds are rushes and reeds.

847   A man of words and not of deeds is like a garden full of weeds.

848   The greatest talkers are least doers.

849   Easier said than done.

850   Empty vessels make the greatest sound.

851   The worst wheel of a cart creaks most.

*　　*　　*

Some words I've said, and cold are my lips as if in the autumn wind.

— *Matsuo Basho*

Tsze-kung asked what constituted a superior man. The Master said, "He acts before he speaks, and afterward speaks according to his actions."

— *Confucius*

The most silent people are generally those who think most highly of themselves.

— *William Hazlitt*

Words that are strictly true seem to be paradoxical.

— *Lao-tzu*

2 BEAUTY

Beauty: its eloquence

852 One hair on a pretty woman's head is enough to tether a great elephant. [*J*]

853 A pretty girl should have an eyebrow like a willow-leaf, an eye like the kernel of an apricot, a mouth like a cherry, a face the shape of a melon seed, and a waist as thin as a poplar. [*C*]

854 How beautiful the girl who looks like a peony when she sits, like a concubine when she stands, and like a lily when she walks. [*J*]

855 Every woman looks prettier in the evening at a distance beneath an umbrella. [*J*]

Western Equivalents

856 Beauty opens locked doors.

857 Beauty draws more than oxen.

858 An enemy to beauty is a foe to nature.

859 A thing of beauty is a joy forever.

Feminine beauty: its shallowness

860 Beauty is but one layer.   [*J*]

861 Underneath the rouge and powder is nothing but a
     skeleton.   [*C*]

862 Nature provides a woman with only three-tenths of
     her beauty.   [*C*]

863 There are many fools among beautiful women.   [*J*]

Western Equivalents

864 Beauty is only skin-deep.

865 Beauty may have fair blossoms, yet bitter fruit.

866 Beauty and folly are often companions.

Feminine beauty: its ill-fatedness and dangers

867 Pretty face, poor fate.   [*C*]

868 It is the beautiful bird which gets caged.   [*C*]

869 Fair maidens are mostly unlucky.   [*C*]

870 A beautiful woman is an axe that cuts off life.   [*J*]

871 Beware of the beautiful woman as you would be of
     the red pepper.   [*J*]

872 The lucky man meets a friend, the unlucky man a
     pretty woman.   [*C*]

Western Equivalents

873 Prettiness dies first.

874 The fairest flower is soonest to fade.

875 The fairest rose ends up withered.

876 Please your eye and plague your heart.

*   *   *

Beauty is its own excuse for being.
— *Ralph W. Emerson*

If beauty makes a display of beauty, it is sheer ugliness. If goodness makes a display of goodness, it is sheer badness.

— *Lao-tzu*

To be born a woman is to know —
Although they do not talk of it at school —
That we must labor to be beautiful.
— *W. B. Yeats*

3 HEART AND MIND

The mind: its importance

877 A mind enlightened is like heaven; a mind in darkness is like hell.   [C]

878 Both glory and hell dwell in the heart. [C]

879 Joy and sorrow exist nowhere but in the heart. [J]

880 Whether one is well or woeful is determined by his mind. [K]

881 Life is either pleasant or painful, depending on how one perceives it. [J]

Western Equivalents

882 The mind is the man.

883 What is man but his mind?

884 Heaven and hell are in your heart.

885 A man is well or woeful as he thinks himself so.

886 There is nothing either good or bad but thinking makes it so.

887 It is the riches of the mind only that make a man rich and happy.

The mind: its changeability and variety

888 A man's mind changes twelve times a day. [K]

889 A man's heart is as changeable as the autumn sky. [J]

890 Ten men, ten minds. [J]

891 Hearts are as unlike as faces. [J]

[878—891]

Western Equivalents

892   A wise man changes his mind, a fool never.

893   Woman's mind and winter's wind change oft.

The human heart: its inscrutable depth

894   Fish in deep waters may be hooked, birds in the sky
       may be shot, but there is no way to grasp the bottom
       of a man's heart.   [C]

895   It is easy to gauge ten fathoms of water, but it is not
       easy to gauge one fathom of a man's heart.   [K]

896   It is possible to measure the depth of a man, but it
       is impossible to measure the depth of a man's heart.
                                                              [J]

       † You can measure the distance inward from the out-
       side of a man's body, but not how deep a man's heart is.

897   It is as difficult to gauge a man's heart as it is to
       chop a duck's gizzard.   [C]

898   Vast chasms can be filled, a man's heart never.   [C]

899   By a long journey we know a horse's strength, and
       length of days shows a man's heart.   [C]

900   If you wish to know a man's heart, listen to his
       words.   [C]

Western Equivalents

901   A man's mind is a dark mirror.

902   The rope that binds thoughts has never been made.

903   One may think who dares not speak.

904   Let no one see what is in your heart or your purse.

905   He who opens his heart surrenders himself as a prisoner.

906   When the heart is full the tongue will speak.

907   The heart's letter is read in the eyes.

908   The book of the heart is read from the eyes.

*   *   *

Nine times in ten the heart governs the understanding.

— *Lord Chesterfield*

Not all those who know their minds know their hearts as well.

— *La Rochefoucauld*

[902 – 908]

4 HAPPINESS

Happiness: its nature and sources

909   Peace in a thatched hut — that is happiness.   [C]

910   So long as there is bread to eat, water to drink and a bended arm to sleep on, happiness is not impossible.
[C]

911   He who goes out of his house in search of happiness runs after a shadow.   [C]

912   Peace is happiness; merit is long life; contentment is wealth; and the obtaining of one's desires is honor.
[C]

913   One can go hungry so long as he can keep his heart at ease.   [K]

914   One with a settled disposition will think even cabbage roots are fragrant.   [C]

915   Happiness and misery are not fated but self-gained.
[C]

916   Joy and sorrow exist nowhere but in the heart.   [J]

[909—916]

Peace in a thatched hut — that is happiness.

917 All happiness in the world arises from a wish for the welfare of others; all misery arises from indulging the self. [C]

918 To the contented even poverty and obscurity bring happiness; to the discontented even riches and honors bring misery. [C]

Western Equivalents

919 Happy is he that chastens himself.

920   Content is happiness.

921   All happiness is in the mind.

922   It is comparison that makes men happy or miserable.

923   Happy is he that is happy in his children.

Happiness: its secrets

924   The three secrets of happiness: see no evil, hear no
       evil, do no evil.   [C]

925   If you would extend the fields of your happiness,
       you must level the soil of your heart.   [C]

926   No money can buy Purity and Leisure.   [C]

927   Happiness is not a horse, so don't try to harness it.
                                                            [C]

928   With half a mat to sit on and one mat to live on,
       one needs nothing more.   [J]

       † "Mat" here refers to an oblong straw mat used as
       flooring in a Japanese house. The implication is that
       to be content with a small livelihood is a secret of
       happiness.

929   All a dead man needs is a space six feet long.   [K]

       † "A space six feet long" refers to a coffin. The im-
       plication is that realization of this simple, grim fact
       will help one to live more honestly and happily.

930   Those without shoes should think of those without
       feet.   [C]

931   Ten thousand dollars cannot purchase a laugh.   [C]

Western Equivalents

932   Let everyone be content with his own level.

933   Humble hearts have humble desires.

934   He that desires but little has no need of much.

935   Let him that would be happy for a day go to the
barber; for a week, marry a wife; for a month, buy
him a new horse; for a year, build him a new house;
for all his lifetime, be an honest man.

936   An ounce of mirth is worth a pound of sorrow.

937   Mirth is the sugar of life.

*   *   *

To describe happiness is to diminish it.
— *Stendhal*

Misery! Happiness is to be found by its side.
Happiness! Misery lurks beneath it. Who knows
what either will come to in the end?
— *Lao-tzu*

If we only wanted to be happy we would be
happy; but we want to be happier than other
people, which is almost always difficult, since we
think them happier than they are.
— *Charles Montesquieu*

CHAPTER FIVE

The Temporal

NO LIVING man can escape time. At his birth, a man finds himself in the sphere of time; he continues to live there until he dies. While he lives, he continues to struggle under the stress of time. It is no wonder that a man should be so deeply concerned with timely events and opportune actions in his life. He hopes that events happen just at a time more useful to himself and that an action will be accomplished at the most advantageous moment. And his fear is that anything short of timeliness or opportuneness may mean to him a source of frustration, failure, and misery. Many proverbs in this section demonstrate people's abiding concern with the element of timeliness in everyday life.

1 TIME

Time: its power

938 A thousand taels will not buy an inch of time. [C]

† "Tael" is a Chinese unit of money.

939 Time is a healer. [K]

940 Wait one hundred years, and most problems will have been resolved. [J]

941 Wisdom is of little avail unless it is in tune with the times. [J]

942 With time and patience the mulberry leaf becomes a silk gown. [C]

943 No man can withstand aging. [J]

Western Equivalents

944 Time is money.

945 Patience, time, and money accommodate all things.

946 Time cures all things.

947 Nature, time, and patience are the three great physicians.

948 Time is a great healer.

949 The crutch of time does more than the club of Hercules.

950 Time devours all things.

Time: its swift flight

951 Time is an arrow, days and months a weaver's shuttle. [C]

952 Time is a swift stream. [K]

953 Time is like the spark of a flint. [K]

954 Time flies like an arrow. [J]

955 Time, may the moth eat thee. [K]

† The devout wish in this proverb is that time, the destroyer of living things, be eaten by moths so that we may avert our fate.

956 Nothing is so easy as the passage of time. [C]

957 Day and night wait for no man. [J]

958 For the busy man time passes quickly. [C]

959 You might dam the flowing waters, but you can never fetch back the days and months. [J]

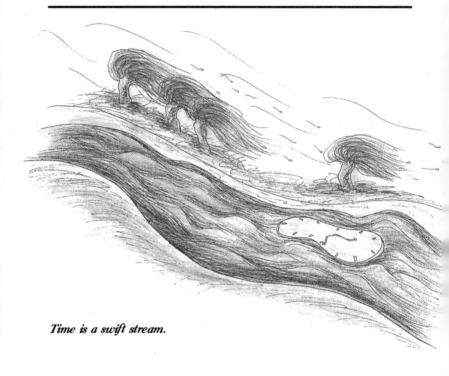

Time is a swift stream.

960   The prime of one's life never returns.   [*J*]

Western Equivalents

961   Time flies.

962   Time has wings.

963   My days are swifter than a weaver's shuttle.

964   Time flees away without delay.

965   Time and tide wait for no man.

966   Things past cannot be recalled.

[960 – 966]

967 Lose an hour in the morning and you'll be all day hunting for it.

968 There are no birds in last year's nests.

*　　　*　　　*

Time: that which man is always trying to kill, but which ends in killing him.
— *Herbert Spencer*

No man is rich enough to buy back his past.
— *Oscar Wilde*

2 OPPORTUNITY

The right time: its value

969 There is a time to cast your nets and a time to mend them. [C]

970 **Waiting brings a good day.** [J]

971 **Even grasshoppers have their day in June.** [K]

† In midsummer, rice plants begin to grow and hordes of grasshoppers swoop down on the rice paddies.

972   Even coarse tea tastes good when freshly brewed.
[*J*]

973   Though grown in the shade, the bean ripens all the same when its time comes.   [*J*]

974   When the melon is ripe it will drop of itself.   [*C*]

Western Equivalents

975   Everything is good in its season.

976   Every dog has his day.

977   There is a time and place for everything.

When the melon is ripe it will drop of itself.

[972–977]

978 Time and straw make medlars ripe.

† The medlar, a fruit that looks like a small brown apple, is eaten when partly decayed.

Seizing the right moment

979 One must not let opportunity slip by. [C]

980 Remove the bull's horns while they are hot. [K]

981 In every worthwhile undertaking, one must do it quick. [J]

982 If heaven drops a date, open your mouth. [C]

983 The gods cannot help a man who misses opportunities. [C]

984 He who can grasp opportunity as she slips by does not need a lucky dream. [C]

985 Make every inch of time your own. [C]

Western Equivalents

986 Know your opportunity.

987 Strike while the iron is hot.

988 Make hay while the sun shines.

989 When fortune smiles, embrace her.

990 Opportunity seldom knocks twice.

99¹   An occasion lost cannot be redeemed.

99²   Take the goods the gods provide.

*   *   *

No great man ever complains of want of opportunity.

— *Ralph W. Emerson*

Next to knowing when to seize an opportunity, the most important thing in life is to know when to forgo an advantage.

— *Benjamin Disraeli*

3 DELAY

Repentance: its worth

993   Repentance is the loveliest of the virtues.   [C]

994   To learn how to write at eighty.   [J]

995   It is never too late to mend the pen after the sheep is lost.   [C]

996   It is never too late to set a dog upon a hare.   [J]

997   Don't hesitate to correct your faults.   [*J*]

Western Equivalents

998   Repentance is not to be measured by inches and hours.

999   Never too late to mend [learn, repent, do well].

1000   Who errs and mends, to God himself commands.

1001   Better late than never.

Warnings against procrastination

1002   To lock the door after the thief has gone.   [*C*]

1003   To mend the barn after the cow is lost.   [*K*]

1004   To make a rope after the thief has sneaked in.   [*J*]
   † The rope is made hopefully to tie and restrain the thief.

1005   To fix the hedge gate after the robbery has taken place.   [*K*]

1006   To fire guns of salute after the general has left on his horse.   [*C*]

1007   To give a prescription after the funeral is over.   [*K*]

1008   To hope in tomorrow is to depend on the cherry blossoms.   [*J*]

† It is not uncommon to see in the morning the cherry trees bereft of their ripened blossoms by the storm overnight. The implication is that it is futile to lay one's hope on uncertain future just as it is useless to expect to see cherry blossoms in their full bloom as long as one wishes.

1009　Better fifty today than one hundred tomorrow. [J]

1010　If you leave the snake half dead, it can still bite. [J]

Western Equivalents

1011　It's too late to shut the stable door after the horse has bolted.

1012　The doctor after death.

1013　After meat, mustard.

1014　Delays are dangerous.

1015　Between two stools you fall to the ground.

1016　Never put off till tomorrow what you can do today.

1017　One hour today is worth two tomorrow.

1018　Never do things by halves.

*　　*　　*

Procrastination is the thief of time.
— *Edward Young*

Excessive scruple is only hidden pride.
— *Goethe*

4 HASTE

Haste or anticipation: its effects

1019　The fool in a hurry drinks his tea with chopsticks.
[C]

1020　A hasty man would sew with the thread tied round the needle's waist. [K]

1021　To set the price for a racoon while it is still in its den. [J]

1022　To borrow money on a fur while the badger is still in its den. [K]

1023　To try to leap while unable to crawl. [K]

1024　To be concerned about the diapers before the child is conceived. [K] [J]

1025　To get the baby's blanket even before getting a spouse. [K]

1026　To wash one's face with the hat already on. [K]

† This is applied to someone moving in haste while getting ready before going out.

The fool in a hurry drinks his tea with chopsticks.

1027 The other person is not even thinking of serving the rice cakes, but you already start drinking the *kimchi* juice.   [K]

† One drinks *kimchi* juice as an appetizer. The implication is of one holding wild expectations before conditions warrant.

Western Equivalents

1028 Marry in haste, and repent at leisure.

[1027 – 1028]

1029 Hasty work, double work.

1030 Haste trips up its heels.

1031 A hasty man never wants woe.

1032 He that passes judgment as he runs, overtakes repentance.

Remedies against haste or anticipation

1033 Haste comes of the evil one, leisure from God. [C]

1034 Giving birth often proves easier than the dreaded anticipation. [J]

1035 There's no medicine that cures care. [K]

1036 A little impatience will spoil great plans. [C]

1037 He who plants a forest in the morning cannot expect to saw planks the same evening. [C]

1038 Can spring come before winter is over? [C]

1039 If you are in a hurry, go round. [J]

1040 Think thrice and do it. [C]

Western Equivalents

1041 Haste is from the devil.

1042 Things are not as black as they look.

1043 Fear of death is worse than death itself.

1044   It is the pace that kills.

1045   Care killed the cat.

1046   Care brings grey hair.

1047   Make haste slowly.

1048   Haste is waste.

1049   The longest way round is the shortest way home.

1050   Look before you leap.

1051   Second thoughts are best.

1052   Don't count your chickens before they are hatched.

1053   Don't sell the skin till you have caught the bear.

*   *   *

Good and quickly seldom meet.
                                        — *George Herbert*

Three things only are well done in haste: flying from the plague, escaping quarrels, and catching flies.
                                        — *H. G. Bohn*

CHAPTER SIX

Practical Concerns

IN HIS struggle for existence, man had deep-rooted desires to have and keep sufficient necessaries of life, such as food, clothing, and shelter. In primitive times when money was not yet in use, such desires were for the things themselves. With the invention of money, however, most of the desires have been directed exclusively to money. Money has become the most important element in all practical concerns of life. In this section we see men taking various views of wealth, a condition in which men have more than enough money for his normal needs and desires, and of poverty, a condition in which men have not enough money for the necessities of life. Also included in this section are other practical concerns of life: health, trade and business, and possession or people's worldly values.

1 WEALTH

Wealth: *its power*

1054   Money can move the gods.   [C] [K]

1055   With money the gods are at your command;
       without it what man can summon another?   [C]

1056   If you have money, all you say is gospel truth. [C]

1057   He who has money can get the devil to turn the
       mill.   [C]

1058   Money is a Hercules.   [K]

1059   No one spits on money.   [K]

1060   Even hell's torments are measured by money.   [J]

       † A reference that the power of money is enormous.
       It is so great that the degree of torment a person will
       suffer in hell is determined by the amount of money
       he offers to the gods.

1061   Even Amida Buddha emits light in proportion to
       the offering.   [J]

1062   With money a dragon, without money a worm. [C]

Even hell's torments are measured by money.

1063   A fool could be a lord if he had money.   [*J*]

1064   To have money is to add on thirty years' dignity.
                                                        [*C*]

   † In former times age often meant added dignity.
   "Thirty years' dignity" means a dignity one would
   enjoy when he has grown older by thirty years.

1065   Money earns money.   [*K*]

1066   No more money, no more relationship.   [*J*]

   Western Equivalents

1067   All things obey money.

1068 A golden key opens every door.

1069 Gold goes in at any gate except heaven's.

1070 Money is the only monarch.

1071 Money makes a man.

1072 Jack would be a gentleman if he had money.

1073 Money talks.

1074 Patience, time, and money accommodate all things.

1075 Money makes money.

1076 Rich folk have many friends.

Riches: their dangers

1077 All money is evil.   [C]

1078 Where there is money, there is danger.   [J]

1079 The money-making corner is a terribly dangerous corner.   [K]

1080 Fish see the bait but not the hook; men see the profit but not the peril.   [C]

1081 Lend money to a good friend, and you'll lose your friend as well as the money.   [K]

1082 Riches take away more pleasures than they give.
                                                      [C]

1083　A busy rich man is like a busy ashtray: they both get dirtier. [K] [J]

Western Equivalents

1084　The love of money is the root of all evil.

1085　Lend your money and lose your friend.

1086　Riches bring care and fears.

1087　Riches rather enlarge than satisfy appetites.

1088　Abundance of things engenders disdainfulness.

1089　The ways to enrich are many, and most of them foul.

The rich and the poor

1090　The rich man thinks of the future; the poor man thinks of the present. [C] [J]

1091　The rich man spends his money, the poor man his strength. [C]

1092　Poor men hover around the fortune-teller's stall, rich men around the medicine cabinet. [C]

1093　The sorrows of the rich are not real sorrows; the comforts of the poor are not real comforts. [C]

1094　Better to be a tight-fisted rich man than an open-handed pauper. [K]

1095   Outwardly a pauper, inwardly a rich man.   [K]

1096   If you are poor, don't cheat; if you are rich, don't presume.   [C]

1097   The rich gather riches; the poor gather years.   [C]

1098   From poverty to profusion is a hard journey, but the way back is easy.   [J]

Western Equivalents

1099   The rich man may dine when he will, the poor man when he may.

1100   Poor men seek meat for their stomach; rich men stomach for their meat.

1101   The rich man has his ice in the summer, and the poor man gets his in the winter.

1102   The pride of the rich makes the labor of the poor.

1103   The pleasures of the mighty are the tears of the poor.

1104   Thr rich follow wealth, and the poor the rich.

1105   Laws grind the poor, and rich men rule the law.

*   *   *

Those who think that wealth is the proper thing for them cannot give up their revenues.

— *Chuang-tzu*

[1095 – 1105]

The best condition in life is not to be so rich as to
be envied nor so poor to be damned.

— *Josh Billings*

Any good practical philosophy must start out with
the recognition of our having a body.

— *Lin Yutang*

To suppose, as we all suppose, that we could be
rich and not behave the way the rich behave, is
like supposing that we could drink all day and stay
sober.

— *L. P. Smith*

2 POVERTY

Poverty: its miseries and dangers

1106 Poverty is worse than four hundred and four
diseases. [*J*]

1107 A dead man is more fortunate than a poor man.[*C*]

1108 The poorer one is, the more devils he meets. [*C*]

1109 Poverty breeds quarrels. [*K*]

1110 Poverty leads to misdeeds. [*K*]

1111 A man without money is like a ship without sails.
[*J*]

[1106 — 1111]

1112 There's no help for the poor even with all the
money in the treasury.   [K]

Western Equivalents

1113 Poverty is the mother of crime.

1114 Lack of money is the root of all evil.

1115 Poverty is the most deadly and prevalent of all
diseases.

1116 Poverty is no vice, but an inconvenience.

1117 The devil dances in an empty pocket.

1118 When poverty comes in at the door, love flies out
of the window.

1119 Poverty breeds strife.

When poverty comes in at the door, love flies out of the window.

[1112–1119]

Poverty: its brighter side

1120 Merry is the beggar that lives in a ditch off the paddy field. [K]

1121 It's the poor who give alms to the poor. [J]

1122 He who can endure in poverty will keep his position when wealthy. [C]

1123 A poor man in his silky attire of indigence. [K]

† This refers to a man of clean integrity no matter how poor he may be financially.

Western Equivalents

1124 He that has no money needs no purse.

1125 Little wealth, little care.

1126 Poverty keeps together more homes than it breaks up.

1127 A ragged coat may cover an honest man.

*　　　*　　　*

Poverty is to be pitied, but impoverishment is a hundred times more pitiable.
— *Jean Paul Richter*

Men feel that cruelty to the poor is a kind of cruelty to animals. They never feel that it is injustice to equals; nay, it is treachery to comrades.
— *G. K. Chesterton*

3 HEALTH

Eating: its importance

1128   Clothes and food are daily mercies.   [C]

1129   We scheme for three meals per day, for one sleep
by night.   [C]

1130   First secure food; then secure clothing.   [C]

1131   Filling one's stomach comes first, and saving one's
face comes next.   [K]

1132   Even a gentleman with a beard three feet long
cannot do without eating.   [K]

† According to Korean tradition, the longer beard a
gentleman had, the greater prestige he enjoyed in society.

1133   No superb views of Mountain Diamond on an
empty stomach.   [K]

† This mountain is well known for its natural
beauty.

Western Equivalents

1134   Bread is the staff of life.

1135 An army marches on its stomach.

1136 The guts uphold the heart, and not the heart the guts.

1137 Stuffing holds out storm.

1138 Better fill a man's belly than his eye.

Rules for good health

1139 For good health, seven parts regimen and three parts medicine. [C]

1140 Regimen first, medicine next. [J]

1141 Few desires, buoyant spirits; many cares, feeble health. [C]

1142 Eat little at dinner, and you may live up to ninety-nine. [C]

1143 No physician is needed for a stomach eight parts full. [J]

1144 Do not covet for the mouth and belly. [C]

1145 The mouth should always consult with the stomach. [C]

1146 Feed moderately on wholesome food; garden herbs surpass rich viands. [C]

1147 Even though your parent has just died, it is still a good thing to rest after your meal. [C] [J]

† The implication is that even in emergency such as your parent's death, you still have to take rest after your meal.

1148 **Those who close their windows to the sun open their doors to the doctor.** [C]

1149 **Keep well covered in spring and delay putting on heavy garments in autumn, and you will hardly ever be sick.** [C]

Western Equivalents

1150 **The best doctors are Dr. Diet, Dr. Quiet, and Dr. Merryman.**

1151 **A little labor, much health.**

1152 **Many dishes make many diseases.**

1153 **Much meat, much malady.**

1154 **Feed by measure and defy the physician.**

1155 **An apple a day keeps the doctor away.**

1156 **After dinner sit awhile, after supper walk a mile.**

1157 **When the sun rises, the disease will abate.**

1158 **Where the sun enters, the doctor does not.**

1159 **A cool mouth, and warm feet, live long.**

Illness: its sources and effects

1160 All illness comes from one's thoughts and feelings.
[J]

1161 When a famous physician comes to the village, everybody has an illness. [C]

1162 Illnesses go in at the mouth; misfortunes come out of the mouth. [C] [J]

1163 A cold is the root of all complications. [J]

1164 He who sits with his back to a draught looks straight into his coffin. [C]

1165 A family that avoids illness for ten years is sure to become rich. [K]

1166 If one has no illness, he is already rich. [K]

1167 Medicine does not kill, the physician kills. [C]

1168 Medicine does not kill, the pharmacist does. [J]

1169 It's the clumsy pharmacist that kills. [K]

1170 Medicine cures the man who is fated not to die.[C]

† If a man is cured of illness, it is not necessarily the medicine but the power of fate working for him.

Western Equivalents

1171 Diseases are the price of ill pleasures.

1172 A May cold is a thirty-day cold.

1173 If cold wind reaches you through a hole, say your prayers, and mind your soul.

1174 A dry cough is the trumpeter of death.

1175 Physicians kill more than they cure.

1176 The doctor is often more to be feared than the disease.

1177 A young physician fattens the churchyard.

*   *   *

Health is not valued till sickness comes.
— *Thomas Fuller*

The soul's maladies have their relapses like the body's. What we take for a cure is often just a momentary rally or a new form of the disease.
— *La Rochefoucauld*

4 TRADE AND BUSINESS

Business: its sense and tactics

1178 In business, affability is a prerequisite.   [C]

1179   A man without a smiling face must not open a
shop.   [C]

1180   When you do business, be as slow and steady as
the cow's slobbering.   [J]

1181   Traders are like priests.   [C]

† Patience is expected of both traders and priests.

1182   The important first three years in business.   [J]

1183   Trade needs haggling as boats need sailing.   [C]

1184   A businessman can no more live all honestly in this
world than a folding screen can stand upright.   [J]

† For a folding screen to stand upright, it must be
partly folded. By the same token, a man must make
some compromise to be a reasonably good businessman.

1185   Great capital, great profits.   [C]

1186   A farmer without an ox; a merchant without capital.   [C]

1187   Great sales but small profits.   [C] [K] [J]

1188   A merchant may complain of loss, yet has a
warehouse built before he knows it.   [J]

1189   A glass of wine in the hand is worth more than a
hundred pending deals.   [C]

1190   Cash at hand is better than a credit to a rich
customer.   [K]

[1179 — 1190]

1191　Eight hundred dollars in ready money is worth more than a thousand dollars of credit. 　[C]

1192　Credit cuts off customers. 　[C]

1193　To give a peck and get a bushel in return. 　[K]

Western Equivalents

1194　The customer is always right.

1195　Slow but steady wins the race.

1196　Keep thy shop, and thy shop will keep thee.

1197　A straight stick is crooked in the water.

1198　Light gains make heavy purses.

1199　To buy and sell, and live by the loss.

1200　It is no sin to sell dear, but a sin to give ill measure.

1201　Weigh justly and sell dearly.

Lending and borrowing

1202　It is easier to capture a tiger in the mountains than to ask for a loan of money. 　[C]

1203　Stand and borrow; kneel and beg the return. 　[C]

† Sometimes the borrower is in a strong position and the creditor in a weak one.

1204 You sit at ease when you lend your money; you stand waiting anxiously when you try to get the money back. [*K*]

1205 He has the face of a Buddhist saint when borrowing; he has the face of a Yama when repaying. [*J*]

† Yama is a Hindu god, judge of the dead and king of the underworld. He usually appears with a scowl.

1206 Lend money to a city, but never to a man. [*J*]

1207 Make a loan to a bad debtor, and he will repay with hate. [*C*]

1208 To throw a fleshy bone at a dog. [*C*]

† To lend money to an unworthy debtor with no prospect of repayment.

1209 If you pelt dogs with meat dumplings, you will lose all and get nothing. [*C*]

1210 Shame fades in the morning, but debts remain from day to day. [*C*]

1211 When the man dies, the debt is lost. [*C*]

1212 The debtor is a culprit before the creditor. [*K*]

1213 The debtor is no less than a slave to the creditor. [*K*]

Western Equivalents

1214 He that goes a-borrowing, goes a-sorrowing.

1215   **The borrower is servant to the lender.**

1216   **A man in debt is caught in a net.**

1217   **Debt is the worst property.**

1218   **Death pays all debts.**

1219   **Neither a borrower nor a lender be.**

The debtor is a culprit before the creditor.

*   *   *

Drive thy business or it will drive thee.
— Benjamin Franklin

Business is really more agreeable than pleasure; it
interests the whole mind, the aggregate nature of
man, more continuously, and more deeply. But it
does not *look* as if it did.
— Walter Bagehot

5   POSSESSION

Possessing life and its accouterments: a worldly view

1220   It is better to linger on the earth than lie beneath
it.   [C]

1221   To be living in this world is still better, even if
you're sleeping on the stable manure.   [K]

1222   Of the Five Blessings, long life is the greatest.   [C]

    † The Five Blessings include long life, wealth,
health, cultivated virtue, and a natural death.

[1220 – 1222]

1223 Rather a live dog than a dead tiger.   [*K*]

1224 Rather a live dog than a deceased premier.   [*K*]

1225 Better a living beggar than a deceased monarch.
    [*C*]

1226 Better a living pauper than a dead millionaire.   [*J*]

1227 Better a premier today than an emperor tomorrow.
    [*K*]

1228 A bird in the soup is better than an eagle's nest in
the desert.   [*C*]

1229 Better are three pennies in my hand than four
hundred dollars in another's.   [*K*]

1230 Fifty today is better than one hundred tomorrow.
    [*J*]

1231 Yen notes in the hand are better than compliments
in the ear.   [*J*]

    † "Yen" is a Japanese unit of money.

1232 The best you can offer to another is something to
fill his belly.   [*K*]

1233 Better a dumpling than a cherry blossom.   [*J*]

1234 A piece of meat is mightier than a thousand
demons.   [*K*]

1235 A grain of rice is mightier than ten demons.   [*K*]

[1223 – 1235]

1236 Where there are many blossoms, there won't be much fruit.   [*J*]

Western Equivalents

1237 Anything is better than nothing.

1238 A feather in the hand is better than a bird in the air.

1239 A bird in the hand is worth two in the bush.

1240 Better a sparrow in the hand than a pigeon on the roof.

1241 Better an egg today than a hen tomorrow.

1242 Praise is not pudding.

1243 Praise fills not the belly.

1244 Praise without profit puts little in the pot.

*   *   *

The great and chief end of men...is the preservation of their property.
— *John Locke*

Property is desirable, is a positive good in the world.
— *Abraham Lincoln*

Worldly faces never look so worldly as at a funeral.
— *George Eliot*

CHAPTER SEVEN

Relationships

NO MAN is an island. To live is to have some sort of relations — in a family, in a marriage, in a social group, whatever. In pre-industrial societies, the worth of an individual was determined more often in terms of the man's status in the family or society. Many of the proverbs listed below may be properly seen from that perspective. This is not to suggest that our way of judging the worth of an individual is now totally different from the way they judged people in pre-industrial societies. Even today family and social relationships remain important factors in a person's life — though with different emphases in different cultures. This section deals with the concerns and customs of those who are joined together by common ancestry and other unifying bonds such as marriage, friendship, and fellowship.

1 FAMILY

The family: its merits and influence

1245 Every man loves his own flesh and blood.   [C]

1246 Every elbow bends inward.   [C] [K]

1247 Brothers are like hands and feet.   [C]

1248 The family that has an old person in it possesses a precious jewel.   [C]

1249 Without old paintings in the hall, a family cannot be said to be established.   [C]

1250 Dragons give birth to dragons, and phoenixes hatch phoenixes.   [C]

† This proverb and the two following proverbs stress the importance of one's family background.

1251 Sow soy beans, and you will reap soy beans; sow red beans, and you will reap red beans.   [K]

1252 No eggplant grows on the melon vine.   [J]

1253 Half of your fortune lies in your family line.   [K]

1254 The splendor of parents sheds its luster sevenfold.

[*J*]

1255 An imbecile basking in his clan's influence.   [*K*]

1256 When there is a rich kinsman in the family, even his cousins partake of the silk gown's warmth.   [*K*]

1257 There's no head of a family who is all idle.   [*K*]

† The implication is that every head of a family does his duty in one form or another, no matter how idle he may appear.

Western Equivalents

1258 Blood is thicker than water.

1259 Like father, like son.

Like father, like son.

1260   Like mother, like daughter.

1261   The birth follows the belly.

1262   The hand that rocks the cradle rules the world.

1263   It is good to be near of kin to land.

1264   Charity begins at home.

Family affairs: how to handle them

1265   Forbearance is the mainspring of a happy home.
                                                                                   [C]

1266   When father and son agree, the family will not fail;
           when brothers agree, the family will not separate.
                                                                                   [C]

1267   Domestic foils must not be spread abroad.   [C]

Western Equivalents

1268   A man should keep from the blind and give to his
           kin.

1269   It's an ill bird that fouls its own nest.

1270   Don't wash your dirty linen in public.

The family: its difficulties

1271   It is easier to rule a kingdom than to regulate a
           family.   [C]

1272   You can't be the head of a family unless you show yourself both stupid and deaf.   [C]

† The head of a family must pretend to be a fool and deaf to minimize the effects of quarrels in the family.

1273   Nobody's family can hang up the sign, "Nothing the matter here."   [C]

1274   Every family cooking pot has one black spot.   [C]

1275   Even the Son of Heaven has his poor relations.   [C]

1276   Brothers are the forerunners of strangers.   [J]

† Unfriendly relationships between brothers eventually produce a generation of strangers.

1277   A good brother is a treasure, a bad brother an enemy.   [K] [J]

1278   In prosperity, strangers claim kin; in adversity, kindred become strangers.   [C]

1279   Children are a perpetual millstone around the neck.   [J]

1280   A father who has married off three daughters sleeps every night with all his doors left open.   [K]

† The dowry was so immense that there is practically nothing left in the house to be robbed.

1281   Parents' shins grow slender as they rear their children.   [J]

1282 Children are children so long as they are in the parents' bosom. [K]

† An implied warning to parents that their children always fall short of their expectations.

1283 Buddha's mercy dwells in the parent's mind and unyielding vehemence in the child's mind. [K]

1284 Parents can hardly guarantee that their offspring will be wise and good. [C]

1285 Parents give their children only their bodies, not their minds. [K]

1286 No man with loyal sons needs money; no money can help a man with false sons. [C]

1287 The least wanted child is one who asks his parents to repay his debt. [K]

1288 It is a bad son who honors his wife more than his mother; it is a bad mother who joins his son in slighting his wife. [C]

1289 It is easier to mine clay with a needle than to build family prosperity; but a family is ruined as easily as the sea destroys a sandcastle. [C]

1290 At the bedside of the chronically ill, where is the filial child? [C]

1291 When the aged parent is long in bed, filial piety is seldom found. [K]

Western Equivalents

1292 Every family has a skeleton in the cupboard.

1293   There is a black sheep in every flock.

1294   Shame in a kindred cannot be avoided.

1295   Many kindreds, much trouble.

1296   Relatives are friends from necessity.

1297   The hatred of the nearest relatives is most intense.

1298   Two daughters and a back door are three arrant thieves.

1299   Children suck the mother when they are young, and the father when they are old.

1300   Children when they are little make their parents fools; when they are great they make them mad.

1301   Children are certain cares, but uncertain comforts.

1302   A little child weighs on your knee, a big one on your heart.

Parents and children: their love and sense of duty

1303   He who has children cannot long remain poor; he who has none cannot long remain rich.   [C]

1304   For the sake of its young the tiger journeys out and back a thousand miles in a single day.   [C]

1305   Children are treasures more precious than a thousand granaries.   [J]

1306   One parent can take care of ten children, but not
ten children one parent.   [K]

1307   If you wish to have children, have three of them. [K]

† Korean parents used to have this curious, but
strong, feeling about having "three" children. This is
no longer true with many Korean parents today; they
now prefer "one" child.

1308   Parents with three children have a happy life.   [J]

† Japanese parents have probably shared this view
with Korean parents. See #1307 above.

1309   The goodness of a father is higher than a mountain,
the goodness of a mother deeper than the sea.   [J]

1310   Never should we dare to injure the bodies that we
received from our parents.   [C] [J]

1311   Good parents ensure their children good marriages;
good children ensure their parents decent burials.
[C]

1312   To try to comfort your parents by covering their
gravestones with blankets.   [J]

† It is useless to try to comfort your parents after
they have passed away.

1313   If you do not care for your parents while they are
alive, there is no point in commemorating them
when they are deceased.   [C]

1314   If you would pray for dutiful children, first be
dutiful to your father and mother.   [C]

1315 Treat your own parents with full filial respect, and you can expect half that from your children.   [K]

1316 The lion that wishes its cub to become a lion abandons it in the valley.   [J]

1317 Strict fathers have filial children.   [C]

1318 If you love your son, give him plenty of cudgels; if you hate him, cram him with dainties.   [C]

1319 Treat the child you love with the rod; treat the child you hate with another cake.   [K]

1320 If you love your son, let him travel on his own. [J]

Western Equivalents

1321 Happy is he that is happy in his children.

1322 The best smell is bread, the best savor salt, the best love that of children.

1323 Children are poor men's riches.

1324 He that has no children knows not what is love.

1325 God and parents and our masters can never be requited.

1326 No love to a father's.

1327 A mother's love is best of all.

1328 A man's mother is his other God.

1329　A mother's love never ages.

1330　One father is enough to govern one hundred sons, but not a hundred sons one father.

1331　One father is more than a hundred schoolmasters.

1332　An ounce of mother is worth a ton of priest.

*　　　*　　　*

For millions of men and women the family is the one and only setting in which human relationships are not governed primarily by considerations of bargaining.

— *Eric L. Mascall*

The best brought-up children are those who have seen their parents as they are. Hypocrisy is not the parents' first duty.

— *G. B. Shaw*

2　MARRIAGE

Marriage: its importance and merits

1333　There are Five Relations, but that of husband and wife stands first.　　　　　　　　　　　　[C]

† The Five Relations generally occur in the following order. Prince and minister; parent and child; husband and wife; elder brother and younger brother; and friends. In the *Yi-Ching* (the Book of Changes) the relation of husband and wife stands first.

1334 A marriage results from pre-natal influences. [C]

1335 Strange is the affinity that binds two in marriage. [J]

1336 The path all good marriages follow: the wife follows the husband. [C]

1337 Husband and wife in perfect accord are like the music of the harp and lute. [C]

1338 In the husband, fidelity; in the wife, obedience. [C]

1339 The husband sings and the wife accompanies. [C]

1340 To live harmoniously as *koto* and *shamisen*. [J]

† *Koto* and *shamisen* are Japanese musical instruments often played together in concert.

1341 Loving husbands and wives enjoy the enduring affection of their sons and daughters. [C]

1342 Many a couple in good marriage looks alike. [J]

† Tradition says that husband and wife in good harmony develop a resemblance to each other.

1343 The needle is always accompanied by the thread. [K]

† The needle here signifies the husband, and the thread the wife.

1344 **The husband is the bucket and the wife is the water jar.** [*K*]

† The husband is the bread-winner, and the wife is the manager of household finances.

1345 **A virtuous wife brings her husband honor; a bad one brings shame.** [*C*]

1346 **A virtuous wife saves her husband from evil ways.** [*C*]

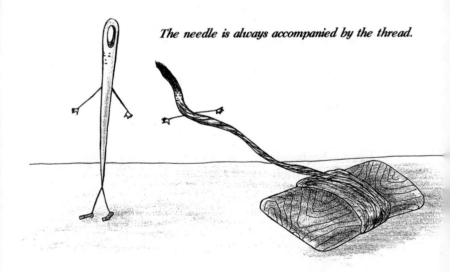

The needle is always accompanied by the thread.

1347   Good-natured and careful – a good wife indeed. [C]

1348   The husband may be ten years older than his wife, but she not a year older than he.   [C]

1349   The husband will never banish from his household the wife who shared all the weal and woe with him.   [C] [K] [J]

Western Equivalents

1350   Marriages are made in heaven.

1351   Love is a flower which turns into fruit at marriage.

1352   Two things do prolong thy life: a quiet heart and a loving wife.

1353   In choosing a wife, and buying a sword, we ought not to trust another.

1354   Choose not a wife by the eye only.

1355   **To live like Darby and Joan.**

   † Darby and Joan, an elderly married couple in an 18th-century folk song, were devoted to each other and lived in perfect harmony.

1356   When the goodman is from home, the goodwife's table is soon spread.

1357   In marriage the husband should have two eyes, and the wife but one.

1358   He that will thrive must ask leave of his wife.

1359   The wife is the key of the house.

Marriage: its difficulties

1360   **Good wives have bad husbands and good husbands have bad wives.**   **[C]**

1361   **Many a divorce derives from cases of mismatch. [J]**

1362   **Nine out of ten go-betweens bear false witness. [C]**

     † The implication is that many go-betweens exagger-
ate. Even today a great many matches are arranged
by the mediation of go-betweens in Asia.

1363   **The husband will ruin his family if he opens his ears too wide to his wife or if he closes his ears too tight.**   **[K]**

1364   **A bad husband is her lifelong enemy; a bad wife is his lifelong enemy.**   **[K]**

1365   **A bad wife is worth one hundred years of bad crops.**   **[J]**

1366   **The three greatest calamities that may befall a man: a flood, a fire, and a bad wife.**   **[K]**

1367   **When calamity wishes to enter a household, it is the wife's tongue that usually provides the staircase.**   **[C]**

1368   **Marriage is something fitted together; it can always come apart.**   **[J]**

1369   **Marriage is an assembly of strangers.**   **[J]**

1370　There's a lid that fits a vessel and there's a lid that doesn't.　　[J]

1371　I'm the pot already wrecked and you're the lid already mended.　　[K]

1372　Horses will not re-mate; men and women will re-marry.　　[C]

1373　Wives and floor-mats are best when they are new and fresh.　　[J]

1374　A wife in command is like a hen crowing in the morning.　　[J]

1375　Never trust a woman, even if she bore you seven children.　　[J]

1376　A married couple's squabbling is like slicing water with a sword.　　[K]

1377　Even dogs won't care to eat the quarrels of a married couple.　　[J]

Western Equivalents

1378　Marriage is a lottery.

1379　The good or ill hap of a good or ill life, is the good or ill choice of a good or ill wife.

1380　Keep your eyes wide open before marriage, and half shut afterward.

1381　Marry in haste, and repent at leisure.

1382 An ill-advised marriage is a spring of misfortune.

1383 He that has a wife has a master.

1384 It is the sorry flock where the ewe bears the bell.

1385 The first wife is matrimony, the second company, the third heresy.

1386 The falling out of lovers is the renewing of love.

*   *   *

Love is an ideal thing, marriage a real thing; a confusion of the real with the ideal never goes unpunished.

— *Goethe*

The most happy marriage I can picture...would be the union of a deaf man to a blind woman.

— *S. T. Coleridge*

Wives can be trained to tolerate their husbands' smoking in bed. This is the surest sign of a happy and successful marriage.

— *Lin Yutang*

$\mathcal{3}$ FRIENDSHIP

Friendship: its importance and merits

1387 If friends have faith in each other, life and death are of no consequence. [C]

1388 It's that strange affinity that knits the bonds of friendship. [J]

1389 True friendship has the taste of water, false friendship the taste of sugary rice drink. [C]

1390 Without a good mirror no lady can know her true appearance; without a true friend not even a scholar can know his own misconduct. [C]

1391 There are three kinds of beneficial friends and there are three kinds of harmful friends. [C]

† The beneficial friends are those who are honest, sincere, and learned. The harmful friends are those who are dishonest, insincere, and have a glib tongue.

1392 Of all kinds of acquaintance, that in which each knows the other's heart is best. [C]

[1387 – 1392]

1393   A relationship in which each lets the other see his own liver and gall-bladder.   [C]

1394   Give me new clothes, but give me old friends.   [C]

1395   As for clothes, the newer the better; as for friends, the older the better.   [K]

1396   There is plenty of yellow gold around, but how many white-haired friends?   [C]

1397   If you spend even a single night with a fellow traveler, erect with him a great wall of ten thousand miles long.   [C] [K]

    † "To erect a great wall" means "to build up a friendship." The expression, "a great wall of ten thousand miles long," is perhaps based on the Great Wall of China.

1398   Running into a good friend abroad is like experiencing rain in a drought.   [C]

1399   Your acquaintances must fill the empire; your close friends must be few.   [C]

1400   Wise men have few friends.   [J]

1401   When good friends become neighbors, they should erect a high fence between them.   [C]

1402   A friend that is made in a year may be lost in an hour.   [C]

1403   Lend money to a good friend, and you will lose the money as well as your friend.   [K]

Western Equivalents

1404 Life without a friend, is death without a witness.

1405 When friends meet, hearts warm.

1406 A friend in need is a friend indeed.

1407 Real friendship does not freeze in winter.

1408 The best mirror is an old friend.

1409 Old friends and old wine and old gold are best.

1410 Have but few friends, though many acquaintances.

1411 Books and friends should be few but good.

1412 A hedge between keeps friendship green.

1413 Friendship increases in visiting friends, but in visiting them seldom.

1414 A friend is not so soon gotten as lost.

1415 Fall not out with a friend for a trifle.

Fellowship: its influence

1416 Keep with good men, and good men you'll imitate; keep with beggars, and outside some gate you'll sleep. [C]

1417 When the character of a man is not clear to you, look at his friends. [J]

1418　**Wormwood surrounded by hemp grows upright of its own accord.** [C] [K] [J]

† Wormwood, usually a slender plant, is able to grow upright when it is surrounded by hemp with its tall, bristly stems.

1419　**If you touch vermillion, you will become of the same color.** [C] [K] [J]

1420　**One dog barks at nothing, and the rest bark at him.** [C]

1421　**Where there's a biting horse, there's a kicking horse, too.** [K]

1422　**If one horse runs wild, the rest of the flock follow suit.** [J]

1423　**One piece of bad meat makes the whole pot smell.** [C]

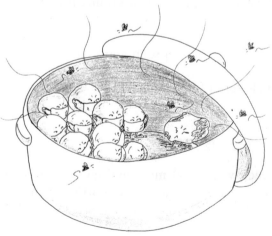

One piece of bad meat makes the whole pot smell.

[1418 – 1423]

1424 It's the hunchback in the company that puts the rest to shame. [K]

1425 One mudfish clouds the whole pond. [K]

1426 Those of a likeness flock together. [C] [K]

1427 A cow likes another cow, and a horse likes another horse. [J]

1428 The crawfish takes sides with the crab. [K]

1429 A black dog takes sides with a pig. [K]

Western Equivalents

1430 A man is known by the company he keeps.

1431 A man is known by his friends.

1432 One rotten apple spoils the barrel.

1433 One scabbed sheep will mar a whole flock.

1434 He that touches pitch shall be defiled.

1435 Who keeps company with the wolf, will learn to howl.

1436 If you lie down with dogs, you will get up with fleas.

1437 Birds of a feather flock together.

1438 A jackdaw always perches by another jackdaw.

1439 Like will to like.

Partnership: its importance and merits

1440   If two men are of one mind, yellow earth can be turned into gold.   [C]

1441   Even a sheet of paper gets lighter when it is carried by two persons.   [K]

1442   In work, the more helpers there are, the better it is.   [J]

1443   Not even robberies work well without helping hands.   [K]

1444   It is difficult to produce a clapping sound with one palm.   [C]

1445   It takes the clap of two hands to make a sound. [K]

1446   A single filament of silk does not make a thread, nor does a single tree make a forest.   [C]

1447   One cannot twist a gimlet with one hand.   [J]

1448   One cannot build a great house with one pole.   [C]

1449   In accommodating others you accommodate yourself.   [C]

1450   If fish are kindhearted, water is also kindhearted.   [J]

1451   If you want to get on in the world, first help others to get on.   [J]

[1440 – 1451]

Western Equivalents

1452   Many hands make light work.

1453   Two hands are better than one.

1454   Three helping one another, bear the burthen of six.

1455   Four eyes see more than two.

1456   One hand washes the other.

1457   Scratch my back and I'll scratch yours.

1458   Scratch my breech and I'll claw your elbow.

Partnership: its difficulties

1459   Too many pilots are bound to sink the ship.   [*C*]

1460   Too many boatmen will drive the boat up the mountain.   [*K*]

1461   Too many oarsmen will strand the boat on the mountain.   [*J*]

1462   Too many carpenters will cause the house to tilt.   [*K*]

1463   Too many monks in the kitchen will break the cooking pots.   [*K*]

1464   If two people keep a horse between them, it will be thin; if two people share a boat, it will leak.   [*C*]

[1452 — 1464]

1465   One man carries two buckets of water for his own use; two men carry one bucket to share between them; three men carry no buckets.   [C]

1466   A single bowl will not produce any sound; but when two are put together, they will go "clang, clang."   [C]

1467   There must be two parties to a quarrel.   [J]

1468   Of three fellow travelers, one is a beggar.   [J]

1469   If the larger beams are crooked, the smaller beams will not be safe, and if the smaller beams are crooked, the house is certain to collapse.   [C]

1470   When a mussel nips the heron's beak, it is the fisherman who profits.   [C] [K] [J]

    † This is based on a Chinese folk tale on the strife between a mussel and a heron. The warning here is that situations of unrest can be exploited by a third party.

1471   When whales fight each other, it is the shrimp whose back gets broken.   [K]

    † The implication is that small people and small nations often suffer at the hands of mighty people and mighty nations. This is one of the lessons that Korea has learned from her bitter experiences with great world powers on the tiny peninsula.

Western Equivalents

1472   Too many cooks spoil the broth.

[1465 – 1472]

1473   In too much dispute truth is lost.

1474   Two is company, three is none.

1475   A crowd is not company.

1476   It takes two to make a quarrel.

1477   Two cats and a mouse, two wives in one house, two dogs and a bone, never agree in one.

1478   Two sparrows on one ear of corn make an ill agreement.

1479   Two dogs strive for a bone, and a third runs away with it.

1480   It is good fishing in troubled waters.

*   *   *

Friendship is almost always the union of a part of one mind with a part of another; people are friends in spots.
— *George Santayana*

Friendship is like money, easier made than kept.
— *Samuel Butler*

=

CHAPTER EIGHT

The Natural

A GOOD deal of human knowledge has derived from man's observation of what goes on in the physical world. In other words, men have learned a great deal from nature in developing their ways of living. This was particularly true when man's dependence on natural facts and forces was greater in pre-industrial societies. This section shows how the peoples of the East and the West have developed their ways and values of decent living in terms of the laws of nature that they thought were at work in the real world.

1 WEATHER AND SEASONS

Weather : its features and effects

1481 **In the morning look toward the southeast, in the evening toward the northwest.** **[C]**

> † The common knowledge shared by farmers is that if the eastern sky glows in the morning, the day will be fine, and if the western sky is red in the evening, the next day will be fine.

1482 **Morning glow, evening rain; sunset glow, sunny weather on the morrow.** **[J]**

1483 **If there is sunset glow, go ahead and whet your scythe for tomorrow.** **[J]**

> † Because the next day is bound to be sunny and good for work in the fields.

1484 **Morning red will bring rain in the evening.** **[K]**

1485 **If the sun glares at its rise, there is a good chance of rain.** **[K]**

1486 **Never rely on the glory of the morning sun nor the smiles of your mother-in-law.** **[J]**

1487   Morning rain is like a woman rolling up her sleeves.
[J]

† "A woman rolling up her sleeves" is not generally taken seriously because her gesture is most likely an empty one.

1488   When it rains about the break of day, the traveler's sorrows pass away.
[C]

1489   When it is bright all round, it will not rain; when it is bright only overhead, it will.
[C]

1490   When the morning mist clears off, the boiling sun cracks the monk's head.
[K]

† A caution to travelers that after a deceptive morning mist the daytime heat usually gets intense.

1491   A rainbow in the east will be followed by a fine day, one in the west by a rainy day.
[C]

1492   If a rainbow rises against the western sky, do not put out your cows at the side of the stream.
[K]

† Because there is going to be a heavy rain.

1493   After a strong gale comes serenity.
[K]

1494   A high wind brings fair weather the next day.
[J]

1495   A halo round the moon is a portent of wind.
[C]

1496   If you see a halo round the moon, you'll have rain in three days or so.
[K]

1497   A plentiful snow presages a good harvest.
[J]

Western Equivalents

1498 Evening red and morning grey help the traveler on his way; evening grey and morning red bring down rain upon his head.

1499 Red sky at night, shepherd's delight; red sky in the morning, shepherd's warning.

1500 If red the sun begins his race, expect that rain will follow apace.

1501 If the sun goes pale to bed, 'twill rain tomorrow, it is said.

1502 Red clouds in the east, rain the next day.

1503 A gaudy morning bodes a wet afternoon.

1504 A cloudy morning bodes a fair afternoon.

1505 Some rain, some rest.

 † To outdoor workers a shower of rain means a short period of relief.

1506 When the mist comes from the hill, then good weather it doth spill; when the mist comes from the sea, then good weather it will be.

1507 If two rainbows appear at one time, they presage rain to come.

1508 If wind follows sun's course, expect fair weather.

1509 Northern wind brings weather fair.

[1498 – 1509]

1510   When the wind is in the west, the weather is at its
       best.

1511   A snow year, a rich year.

1512   Under water, famine; under snow, bread.

Spring: its features and effects

1513   Spring is sooner recognized by common plants than by
       men.   [C]

1514   A man prays to his god as the grass waits for spring.
                                                             [C]

1515   It is spring when the gayest colors abound.   [C]

*Spring is sooner recognized by
common plants than by men.*

1516   **When spring comes every spot is perfumed with flowers.** [C]

1517   **Three days not having looked at the world, and lo, it is full of cherry blossoms!** [J]

   † The blooming of cherry blossoms heralds the beginning of spring in Japan.

1518   **Every spring withered trees blossom, but what man is young twice?** [C]

1519   **Like the spring breeze blowing all around.** [C] [K] [J]

   † This figure of speech is often used to refer to a goodhearted, agreeable man making himself universally welcome as a spring breeze.

1520   **In spring the slumberer knows not the coming of dawn.** [C] [K] [J]

   † The night is so short in spring that one is apt to sleep into the late hours of the morning.

1521   **Spring has a stepmother's face.** [C]

   † Spring is as changeable as a stepmother's countenance and as unpredictable as her moods.

1522   **A woman's heart is as changeable as spring weather.** [J]

1523   **Spring cold is as short-lived as an old man's health.** [C] [K]

1524   **Never to be feared are the spring snow and the toothless wolf.** [J]

[1516–1524]

1525   **Even the spring blossom has its day.**   **[K]**

 † The spring blossom is generally considered short-lived.

1526   **A man tanned in the spring sun is hardly recognized even by his lover.**   **[K]**

 † One gets a darker tan from the spring sun.

1527   **Frequent rains in spring are just as harmful as the extravagant manners of a farmer's wife with crops in autumn.**   **[K]**

Western Equivalents

1528   **When the cuckoo comes, he eats up all the dirt.**

 † The arrival of the cuckoo announces the end of the foul, wintry weather and heralds the beginning of spring.

1529   **The swallow starts the spring and the nightingale finishes it.**

1530   **When you can tread on nine daisies at once, spring has come.**

 † Spring is here when you can tread on nine daisies at once on the village green.

1531   **There's no time like spring, when life's alive in everything.**

1532   **No autumn fruit without spring blossoms.**

1533   **In the spring a young man's fancy lightly turns to thoughts of love.**

† A line immortalized by Alfred Lord Tennyson.

1534 **Love, whose month is ever May.**

† From Shakespeare's *Love's Labour's Lost*.

1535 **April showers bring forth May flowers.**

1536 **A cold April gives bread and wine.**

† Cold weather in April was regarded as good fortune by farmers.

1537 **The spring is not always green.**

1538 **Woman is as fickle as April weather.**

1539 **A May flood never did good.**

Summer: its features and effects

1540 **In the hot summer sun even the shade of a passing hawk helps.** [*K*]

1541 **The bull's horns come off in the heat of summer.** [*K*]

1542 **Summer heat and winter cold last only till the equinox.** [*J*]

† Summer heat and winter cold are short-lived. This is said to someone complaining about extremes in temperature. The vernal equinox (March 21) generally marks the end of cold weather, while the autumnal equinox (September 23) marks the end of sultry weather.

1543   When the weather is hot and hard to bear, we pursue the breeze for a little fresh air.   [*C*]

1544   A guest coming in summer is more dreadful than a tiger.   [*K*]

    † It is extremely hard to entertain guests in summer weather.

1545   A summer shower may soak a horse's right ear, but not his left ear.   [*K*]

    † The summer shower falls in random spots.

1546   A summer shower parts the mane of a horse.   [*J*]

    † Synonymous with #1545 above.

1547   A summer rain after the heat; an autumn rain after the cold.   [*K*]

Western Equivalents

1548   Look for summer on the top of an oak tree.

    † The sprouting of the oak tree heralds the beginning of summer.

1549   Summer is a seemly time.

1550   Summer's parching heat.

1551   Summer has set in with its usual severity.

1552   An English summer, two fine days and a thunderstorm.

1553   There is something of summer in the hum of insects.

1554   Summer will not last forever.

1555   A dry summer never made a dear peck.

> † It is said that in such years the grain is good and hearty, even though the straw is short.

Autumn: its features and effects

1556   When a leaf of the paulownia falls, every one knows it is autumn.   [C]

> † The paulownia is a Chinese tree of the figwort family.

1557   With the fall of one leaf we know that autumn has come to the world.   [J]

1558   High sky, fat horses.   [C] [K]

> † In autumn the sky is typically so clear that it seems higher than ever, and the farmer's horses become fat because there is plenty of grain.

1559   Autumn high, horses fat.   [J]

1560   The autumn sky changes seven and a half times.   [J]

> † A reference to the changeable nature of fall weather.

1561   An autumn day is as short as a deer's tail.   [K]

[1553 – 1561]

1562 The autumn sun sinks as fast as a bucket into a well. [J]

1563 In autumn even the kitchen poker moves busily. [K]

† The whole farm household, including the kitchen poker, is busily occupied in autumn.

1564 In autumn a married woman in need had better go to the harvest field than to her destitute parents' home. [K]

1565 In autumn a married woman in need had better go to the harvest field than to her former nanny. [J]

1566 In autumn even the nails on your fingers and toes enjoy eating. [K]

† Everyone has a good appetite in autumn.

1567 The moon of mid-autumn is exceedingly bright. [C]

1568 The deer of autumn come at the sound of the flute. [J]

† Autumn is the mating season, and in this proverb male deer are compared to lovesick men.

1569 On the ninth month's *ching yang* ("double yang") all want to gather around the household fire. [C]

† All odd numbers are *yang* in Chinese, so *ching yang* mean the ninth day of the ninth month in the lunar calendar.

Western Equivalents

1570 Some of us call it autumn, and others call it God.

1571   **Earth's crammed with heaven, and every common bush afire with God.**

    † A line immortalized by Elizabeth B. Browning.

1572   **Autumn, the fairest season of the year.**

1573   **Of fair things the autumn is fair.**

1574   **When fern grows red, then milk is good with bread.**

    † People used to believe that milk is thicker in autumn than in summer.

1575   **Fruit-bearing autumn.**

1576   **No autumn fruit without spring blossoms.**

1577   **No tree bears fruit in autumn that does not blossom in the spring.**

Winter: its features and effects

1578   **Nobody complains over a hundred fine days in winter.**   [C]

1579   **After the winter solstice, days lengthen and a thread may be added.**   [C]

    † More work, such as a weaver's, may be done in winter.

1580   **When it snows in flakes of six leaves, expect a prosperous year.**   [C]

1581   **A plentiful snow presages a good harvest.**   [J]

[1571 – 1581]

1582   **The day after a snowfall is the beggar's laundry day.**   **[K]**

> † It is usually sunny and warm this day.

1583   **The day after a snowfall the pauper washes his clothes.**   **[J]**

Western Equivalents

1584   **One woodcock does make a winter.**

1585   **Every mile is two in winter.**

1586   **Winter eateth what summer getteth.**

1587   **Winter draws out what summer laid in.**

1588   **Winter thunder, summer hunger.**

1589   **Winter's thunder and summer's flood never boded Englishmen good.**

1590   **After a rainy winter follows a fruitful spring.**

1591   **Sunny winter, a plentiful harvest.**

1592   **A good winter brings a good summer.**

1593   **A green winter makes a fat churchyard.**

> † There is no absolute truth in this proverb. A good many proverbial observations on the seasons of the year are groundless.

*   *   *

There is nothing more universally commended than a fine day; the reason is, that people can commend it without envy.

— *William Shenstone*

Spring is a virgin, Summer a mother, Autumn a widow, and Winter a stepmother.

— *Polish Proverb*

Each season has its ending and beginning; each age has its changes and transformations; misery and happiness regularly alternate.

— *Chuang-tzu*

2 CAUSE AND EFFECT

Cause or origin: its importance

1594   Everything must have a cause.   [C]

1595   Rivers have sources; trees have roots.   [C]

1596   There are no waves if there is no wind.   [C]

1597   There are no leaves on a rootless tree.   [K]

[1594—1597]

1598	No root, no tree.	[K]
1599	No hide, no hair.	[K]
1600	No sleep, no dreams.	[K]
1601	You may see the man in the boy.	[C]
1602	Sandalwood is fragrant even from the seedling.	[K]
1603	From the pure spring comes the pure stream.	[K]
1604	When the head moves, the tail will do likewise.	[J]
1605	Every man gets what he cultivates.	[C]
1606	He who sows hemp will reap hemp; he who sows beans will reap beans.	[C]
1607	Sow melons, and you will reap melons.	[C]
1608	Sow soy beans, and you'll reap soy beans; sow red beans, and you'll reap red beans.	[K]
1609	No eggplant grows on the melon vine.	[J]
1610	You can never steal a child from its stock.	[K]
1611	A chicken cannot turn into a phoenix.	[K]
1612	Give a crow a hundred baths, but it will never turn into a heron.	[J]
1613	Let a white frog live in a chimney for three years, and it will remain a white frog all the same.	[K]

Sow soy beans, and you'll reap soy beans;
sow red beans, and you'll reap red beans.

1614 Happiness has its foundation, misery its womb. [C]

1615 Only the mighty mountains have deep valleys. [K]

1616 If the mountains are lofty, the valleys are bound to
be deep. [J]

1617 Only in the deep woods do goblins lurk. [K]

Western Equivalents

1618 Everything has its seed.

1619 There's no smoke without fire.

1620 Where there are reeds, there is water.

[1614 – 1620]

1621   No root, no fruit.

1622   Take away the cause and the effect will cease.

1623   Eagles do not breed doves.

1624   You may not expect a good whelp from an ill dog.

1625   You reap what you sow.

1626   As you sow, so you reap.

1627   Like father, like son.

1628   Like good leader, like good soldier.

1629   Such beef, such broth.

1630   You can't make a silk purse out of a sow's ear.

1631   The leopard cannot change his spots.

1632   Scratch a Russian, and you will find a Tartar.

1633   You cannot make a crab walk straight.

A beginning: its importance and effects

1634   A good beginning is the most important thing.   [*J*]

1635   To have begun is half done.   [*K*]

1636   The highest towers begin from the ground.   [*C*]

1637   The climbing of a height begins from the base.   [*J*]

1638   A journey of a thousand miles begins with one single step.   [*C*] [*K*]

1639   No monk begins his career as head of a temple. [*J*]

1640   The man who removed a mountain was he who began carrying away the small stones.   [*C*]

1641   He who makes the first false move is certain to lose the game.   [*C*] [*K*] [*J*]

1642   To start off with the head of a tiger and to end with the tail of a snake.   [*C*]

1643   To start off with the head of a dragon and to end with the tail of a snake.   [*K*]

1644   When the start is too good, it sometimes leads to a bad ending.   [*J*]

Western Equivalents

1645   A good beginning makes a good ending.

1646   Well begun is half done.

1647   The first blow is half the battle.

1648   Such beginning, such ending.

1649   An ill beginning, an ill ending.

1650   A good beginning, but a poor finish.

1651   To start off with a bang and to end with a whimper.

[1638 – 1651]

1652   A good salad may be the prologue to a bad supper.

Agent and fulfillment

1653   Nothing good has ever been achieved without great effort and opposition.   [C]

1654   Successful men are seldom easygoing, and easygoing men are seldom successful.   [C]

1655   The course of true love never did run smooth.   [C]

1656   It takes a long time to complete a large vessel.
                                                    [C] [K] [J]

        † "A large vessel" here refers to a man of superior character.

1657   Without climbing the mountain how do you expect to see the plain?   [J]

1658   A gem is not polished without rubbing, nor a man perfected without trials.   [C]

1659   Three bushels of beads make no jewels until they are strung together.   [K]

1660   By hard work Yu Kung succeeded in moving two mountains to open a road.   [C]

        † Yu Kung's success story is based on an ancient Chinese legend.

1661   Ice does not freeze on the busy spinning wheel. [K]

1662	A pagoda built with great effort will hardly go wasted. [K]

| 1663 | Even Heaven cannot stop a diligent man from getting rich. [K] |

| 1664 | The harder one works, the more he will get. [K] |

| 1665 | One idle day in the summer, ten hungry days in the winter. [K] |

| 1666 | With single-minded devotion, anything can be achieved in this world. [C] [K] [J] |

| 1667 | One sincere thought can move both Heaven and Earth. [C] [K] |

| 1668 | Heaven hears even the wishes of an ant. [J] |

| 1669 | What tree will not fall to ten attempts at felling it? [K] |

| 1670 | An arrow shot with determined will can pierce a stone. [C] [J] |

| 1671 | Firm resolution sends even a demon flying. [J] |

| 1672 | When the melon is ripe, it will drop of itself. [C] |

| 1673 | Ripe melons drop without plucking. [J] |

| 1674 | Many a small stream makes a mighty ocean. [C] |

| 1675 | Tiny ants build a mighty tower. [K] |

[1662 – 1675]

1676   When dust accumulates, it will make a big mountain.
[*K*] [*J*]

Western Equivalents

1677   Success does not come overnight.

1678   Rome was not built in a day.

1679   Where bees are, there is honey.

1680   He that would have the fruit must climb the tree.

1681   No sweet without sweat.

1682   No pains, no gains.

1683   Ninety percent of inspiration is perspiration.

1684   Where there's a will, there's a way.

1685   Nothing is impossible to a willing mind.

1686   An idle youth, a needy age.

1687   They must hunger in frost that will not work in heat.

1688   Many a little makes a mickle.

1689   Many drops make a shower.

Absence: its effects

1690   The absent one gets farther away every day.   [*J*]

[1676 – 1690]

1691 Three years after a family has been divided, its
members become like neighbors. [C]

1692 After ten years, even the hills and rills are no
longer what they used to be. [K]

1693 Once away from the parents' bosom, the children
are no longer the parents'. [K]

1694 When a man is away from home, his life is all
sorrow and uneasiness. [K]

1695 Not meeting with another, one's heart grows even
tenderer. [J]

Western Equivalents

1696 Long absent, soon forgotten.

1697 Out of sight, out of mind.

1698 Seldom seen, soon forgotten.

1699 What escapes the eyes is no longer in the heart.

1700 Far from home, near thy harm.

1701 Absence makes the heart grow fonder.

1702 Absence sharpens love, presence strengthens it.

1703 Friends agree best at a distance.

[1691 – 1703]

Absence of the mighty: its effects

1704   The monkeys go wild in the mountains when there is no king in control.   [C]

1705   When the tiger is away, the rabbit is master.   [K]

1706   When the big horse is away, the small horse will take command.   [K]

1707   When eagles doze, little birds twitter.   [J]

1708   To refresh yourself doing the laundry while the demon is away.   [J]

† "Doing the laundry" here probably refers to free, leisurely activity.

Western Equivalents

1709   When the cat's away the mice will play.

1710   Well kens the mouse when the cat's out of the house.

*   *   *

All human actions have one or more of these seven causes: chance, nature, compulsion, habit, reason, passion, desire.

— *Aristotle*

If you miss the first buttonhole, you will not succeed in buttoning up your coat.

— *Goethe*

3 COMPARISON AND CONTRAST

Great and small

1711   Though it may be great, it is always so in comparison to something.   [C]

1712   Each house has its long and its short; each door has its high and its low.   [C]

1713   Some fingers are long and others are short, even though they were born at the same hour on the same day.   [K]

1714   Because there are fools, wise men look well.   [J]

1715   If one month is long, another month is shorter.   [K]

1716   There are some who run overland and there are some who fly above.   [K]

1717   To the ant a few drops of rain are a flood.   [J]

1718   The higher the mountain is, the deeper its valleys are.   [K]

1719   The mightier the mountain is, the longer shadows it casts.   [K]

[1711 – 1719]

*There are some who run overland and
there are some who fly above.*

1720   The deeper the water is, the more fish it draws. [*K*]

1721   The higher the branches in a tree, the more easily
       they break in the wind.   [*K*]

1722   The greater a tree is, the more easily it breaks in
       the wind.   [*J*]

[1720 – 1722]

1723 The more branches a tree has, the more winds it attracts. [*K*]

1724 Better be the beak of a hen than the rump of an ox. [*C*] [*J*]

1725 Better be the comb of a rooster than the tail of a cow. [*K*]

1726 Better be the head of a hen than the tail of a dragon. [*K*]

1727 Rather than the head of a sardine, be the tail of a sea bream. [*J*]

† This is antonymous with the three proverbs above.

1728 An anthole may break down a huge embankment. [*C*] [*K*] [*J*]

1729 Great boats are afraid of little leaks. [*C*]

1730 You think it's only a drizzle, but the small drops drench you in no time. [*K*]

Western Equivalents

1731 It is comparison that makes men happy or miserable.

1732 Talent above talent.

1733 The fox knows much, but more he that catches him.

1734 No man so good, but another may be as good as he.

1735   Great winds blow upon high hills.

1736   The highest tree has the greatest fall.

1737   Choose rather to be the tail of a lion than the head of a fox.

1738   It's better to be first in a village than second in Rome.

1739   Better be the head of a dog than the tail of a lion.

1740   A small leak will sink a great ship.

1741   Many drops make a shower.

Youth and age

1742   Just as wave succeeds wave on the Yangtze River, so young men succeed older men on the land.   [C]

1743   Every spring withered trees blossom, but what man is young twice?   [C]

1744   We remember riding on bamboos as boys, and lo, we are white with age.   [C]

1745   A little boy may soon become old before learning enough.   [J]

1746   Do not laugh at another for having grown old, for that will assuredly happen to you.   [C]

1747   Treat every old man as thy father.   [J]

1748 If deferential to experienced old men, you can rely on them when you are perplexed. [C]

1749 Ignore an old man's advice and one day be a beggar. [C]

1750 If you want to know how to get on, ask the advice of three old people. [C]

1751 He must err grievously who won't listen to aged men. [C]

1752 In old age, take heed to what your children have to say. [C] [K]

1753 A man of eighty years has something to learn from a child of three. [K]

1754 To learn from the child borne on your back. [K]

1755 To wade a ford, guided by the child borne on your back. [J]

1756 The old often forget; the young are often thoughtless. [J]

1757 Inferior in youth, useless in old age. [C]

Western Equivalents

1758 Young men may die, but old men must die.

1759 If you wish good advice, consult an old man.

1760 If the counsel be good, no matter who gave it.

[1748—1760]

1761   Youth has a beautiful face, old age a beautiful soul.

1762   There would be miracles if youth could know and age could do.

1763   If youth knew! If age only could!

1764   A young trooper should have an old horse.

1765   A pious youth, an old-age devil.

1766   You cannot put an old head on young shoulders.

Pleasure and pain

1767   When joy is extreme, it is the forerunner to grief.
[C]

1768   Pleasure is the seedbed of pain; pain is the seedbed of pleasure. [J]

1769   Where there is comfort, there is pain. [J]

1770   He who toils with pain will eat with pleasure. [C]

1771   Disaster sometimes rolls over and becomes blessing.
[C] [K]

Western Equivalents

1772   Pleasure must be purchased with the price of pain.

1773   Sorrow and gladness succeed each other.

1774   Sorrow is at parting if at meeting there be laughter.

1775   Short pleasure, long lament.

1776   Sweet is pleasure after pain.

*   *   *

I shall go out with the chariots to counsel and
command, for that is the privilege of the old; the
young must fight in the ranks.

— *Homer*

Pleasure and pain are the only springs of action in
man, and always will be.

— *C. A. Helvetine*

Perception of what is small is [the secret of]
clear-sightedness; the guarding of what is soft and
tender is [the secret of] strength.

— *Lao-tzu*

4 APPEARANCE AND REALITY

Dress: its value and effects

1777   Dress makes the gentleman or lady.   [C]

1778   Man, like a tree, depends on his clothing.   [C]

[1775 — 1778]

1779 As a house needs men to set it off, so a man needs clothes. [*C*]

1780 Three-tenths of good looks are due to nature, seven-tenths to dress. [*C*]

1781 Nearly seventy percent of life is a matter of appearances. [*J*]

1782 Your clothes are your robe of feathers. [*K*]

1783 A poorly-fed stomach is unseen, but a poorly-dressed body is readily seen. [*K*]

1784 Making a show of oneself is a necessary art of living. [*J*]

1785 Though in tatters at home, one must be in silk abroad. [*J*]

1786 Judge a horse by its saddle, a man by his clothes. [*C*]

1787 Even a metal stake is good-looking when it is dressed up. [*K*]

1788 Even a stump looks good when it is dressed up. [*J*]

1789 A well-dressed whore has less difficulty entering a temple than ten honest women in rags have of visiting the house of a respectable man. [*C*]

Western Equivalents

1790 Apparel makes the man.

1791   The tailor makes the man.

1792   Fine feathers make fine birds.

1793   A fair face cannot have a crabbed heart.

1794   Dress up a stick, and it does not appear to be a stick.

1795   Go well clad, for a stake well dressed seems not to be so.

Even a stump looks good when it is dressed up.

Appearance: its value

1796   What is truly within will be manifested without. [C]

1797   A man's face reflects his state of mind.   [C]

1798   A good-looking cake has a good taste.   [K]

1799   Fair without, fair within; foul without, foul within.   [K]

1800   It is by its blossom that the cherry tree stands out among others.   [J]

1801   A pretty girl should have an eyebrow like a willow leaf, an eye like the kernel of an apricot, a mouth like a cherry, a face like the shape of a melon, and a waist as thin as a poplar.   [C]

1802   A man's eye should be as thin and as straight as a thread, a coward's as big and as round as a bell.   [C]

1803   When a man courts a woman, self-confidence is the most important thing; then money; then his appearance.   [C]

Western Equivalents

1804   An honest look covereth many faults.

1805   A beautiful face is a silent commendation.

1806   Personal beauty is a greater recommendation than any letter of recommendation.

1807   There is a great deal in the first impressions.

Appearance: its deceptiveness

1808   To judge a man from his face is as hard a feat as it
        would be to mete the ocean in pecks.   [C]

1809   You cannot judge a person by his looks.   [J]

1810   Beauty is only one layer.   [J]

1811   Outwardly a virtuous gentleman, inwardly a petty
        man.   [C]

1812   A pauper in fact, a millionaire in aspect.   [K]

1813   A beast wearing man's clothes and hat.   [C]

1814   The face belies the heart.   [J]

1815   He hangs a sheep's head, and sells dog's meat.
                                        [C] [K] [J]

1816   The "dog apricot" often looks luscious.   [K]

        † The "dog apricot" is a wild fruit that tastes sour
        and puckery.

1817   The more flowers a tree has, the less fruit it bears.
                                                    [J]

1818   There isn't much to eat at the much-rumored feast.
                                                    [K]

1819   Cotton clothes, silky heart.   [J]

[1807 – 1819]

1820   An old man may have a youthful heart; a poor man may have a noble inclination.   [C]

1821   Horses and warriors are alike: they are not always what they seem to be.   [J]

1822   The crow's feather is black, but no so its flesh. [K]

1823   The priest from afar best reads the ritual.   [C]

† People tend to idealize the priest from a distance as they do with many other objects with which they are not familiar.

1824   Other people's wives are best.   [C]

1825   The cake on another's plate always looks bigger.   [K]

1826   The beans in another's rice bowl always look bigger.   [K]

1827   Flowers are always red and bright in our neighbor's garden.   [J]

1828   The wheat cooked in our neighbor's kitchen tastes better than the rice cooked in our own.   [J]

† In normal circumstances most Asians think rice to be more delectable than wheat.

Western Equivalents

1829   All that glitters is not gold.

1830   Never judge from appearances.

1831   None can guess the jewel by the casket.

1832   You can't tell a book from its cover.

1833   He cries wine, and sells vinegar.

1834   Beauty may have fair leaves, yet bitter fruit.

1835   Fair face, foul heart.

1836   The grass is always greener on the other side of the fence.

1837   Our neighbor's cow gives more milk than ours.

1838   Far fowls have fair feathers.

1839   Blue are the faraway hills.

*   *   *

Things are seldom what they seem. Skim milk masquerades as cream.
— *W. S. Gilbert*

It is only shallow people who do not judge by appearances.
— *Oscar Wilde*

5 LIVING AND DYING

Life: its brevity

1840   Life is just like the morning dew.   [C]

1841   A man's life is as fragile as the morning dew.   [J]

1842   A man's life is just like that of a fly.   [K]

1843   Life is like a dew drop on a leaf of grass.   [K]

1844   Life hanging by a single thread.   [K]

1845   Man's life is like a candle in the wind, or hoarfrost on the tiles.   [C]

1846   Red faces in the morning, white bones at night. [J]

1847   Man's life on earth resembles a spring dream; when the soul has fled, all is over.   [C]

1848   Few have ever attained the age of threescore years and ten.   [C]

1849   Suppose you are one hundred years of age, you have lived only 36,000 days.   [K]

[1840 – 1849]

Life hanging by a single thread.

1850 Man lives a generation as plants live a spring. [C]

1851 A generation is like a swift horse passing a crevice. [C]

1852 Men live like birds in a wood together; but when the set time comes each takes his flight. [C]

[1850 – 1852]

Western Equivalents

1853   Life is but a span.

1854   Life is a shadow.

1855   Life is a shuttle.

1856   Art is long, life is short.

1857   Life runs as fast as a chariot's wheel.

1858   Life is half spent before we know what it is.

1859   My days are swifter than a weaver's shuttle.

Life: its ups and downs

1860   Life's ups and downs turn like a spinning wheel.
       [K]

1861   When the bitters of adversity are exhausted, then
       come the sweets of happiness.   [C]

1862   There is an uphill road and there is a downhill
       road.   [J]

1863   Life's journey is that of a wayfarer.   [K]

1864   Life is a long journey taken with heavy packs on
       one's back.   [J]

1865   The sunny side can become the shady side, and the
       shady side the sunny side.   [K]

1866   The sunbeam sometimes streams even into a mousehole. [*K*]

1867   Dew drops sometimes fall on the fields littered with dog dung. [*K*]

1868   After a high mountain, a plain comes into view. [*K*]

1869   After a rain the ground becomes firm. [*K*] [*J*]

† Good comes out of bad. For example, after a quarrel comes a renewed friendship; and violent storms make trees take deeper root.

Western Equivalents

1870   Life has its ups and downs.

1871   Life is a pilgrimage.

1872   Life is not all beer and skittles.

1873   Life means strife.

1874   The life of man is a winter's day and a winter's way.

1875   He that falls today may rise tomorrow.

1876   The darkest hour is that before the dawn.

1877   After a storm comes a calm.

1878   A foul morning may turn to a fair day.

Death: inevitable, immanent, and implacable

1879 No mortal escapes death. [C] [K] [J]

1880 Man has no better idea of when he will die than a cart has of when it will be upset. [C]

1881 Death comes to young and old alike. [C] [K] [J]

1882 No such thing as "young" and "old" in the realm of death. [K]

1883 On the road to Hades no traveler is too young or too old. [J]

1884 The blunt axe can be sharpened, but the dead man can never return to life. [K]

1885 The fallen blossom never returns to the branch; the shattered mirror never again reflects. [C] [J]

1886 As time goes, grey hair comes. [K]

1887 White hair is Death's harbinger. [J]

1888 To die is not much sorrow; to waste away to death is the real sorrow. [K]

1889 The fear of death is the beginning of discipline. [C]

Western Equivalents

1890 All men are fated to die.

1891 Nothing so sure as death.

1892   Death is the line that marks the end of all.

1893   Death keeps no calendar.

1894   Death takes no bribes.

1895   All who live must die, and none who die can
renew their life on earth.

Life and death

1896   To be born is in the course of nature, but to die is
according to the decrees of destiny.   [C]

1897   There is a day to be born and a day to die.   [C]

1898   When marked out by destiny, a man will assuredly
drown even though he lives his whole life among
the highest branches of a date tree.   [C]

1899   Living is a spring dream, dying like going back
home.   [C]

1900   When a man's lifework is done, he leaves empty-
handed.   [C]

1901   Man brings nothing at birth, and at death takes
nothing away.   [C]

1902   A dying leopard leaves his skin, a dying man his
name.   [C] [K] [J]

1903   After death, most men are spoken well of.   [J]

[1892 – 1903]

1904   As the eagle's call echoes in the mountains, so a
       man's name continues after his death.   [C]

Western Equivalents

1905   It is natural to die, as to be born.

1906   Dying is as natural as living.

1907   Dust thou art, and unto dust shalt thou return.

1908   Death squares all accounts.

1909   Death acquits us of all obligations.

1910   A good life hath but few days, but a good name
       endureth forever.

*   *   *

Thou canst not judge the life of man until death
hath ended it.
                                  — *Sophocles*

Teach me to live, that I may dread
The grave as little as my bed.
                         — *Bishop Thomas Ken*

Man at his birth is supple and weak; at his death,
firm and strong. So it is with all things.... It is that
firmness and strength that are the concomitants of
death; softness and weakness, the concomitants of
life.
                                   — *Lao-tzu*

CHAPTER NINE

The Supernatural

SCIENCE AS we know it today is an outgrowth of man's search for knowledge based on facts and laws in orderly systems of the universe. This is a relatively modern phenomenon. Prior to this, the peoples of the East and the West had been accustomed to seeing certain agencies, influences, and phenomena above or beyond what is natural. This section illustrates some of the most important concepts and expressions that characterized the supernatural habits of mind in the earlier centuries of human history. Some of the old proverbs given here are far from true when viewed from a scientific standpoint, but they will serve as useful means of understanding some of the ways and values of pre-industrial societies.

1 HEAVEN AND FATE

Heaven: omniscient and provident

1911   What man sees not and knows not, Heaven sees and knows.   [C]

1912   Nothing can escape the eye of Heaven.   [C]

1913   God sees through everything.   [J]

1914   You may deceive men; you can't deceive Heaven.   [C] [K]

1915   Sins committed in the dark are seen in Heaven like sheets of fire.   [C]

1916   A thousand human schemes may be thwarted by one scheme of Heaven.   [C]

1917   It is man's to scheme; it is Heaven's to accomplish.   [C]

1918   Man depends on Heaven as a ship on her pilot. [C]

1919   Our daily bread depends on Heaven.   [C]

1920   When men have good desires, Heaven is sure to further them.   [C]

1921   Heaven stands by a good man.   [C]

1922   Without the assistance of Heaven, man cannot
       walk an inch.   [C]

1923   He who follows Heaven will prosper; he who acts
       against Heaven will perish.   [J]

1924   The will of the people is the will of Heaven. [C] [K]

1925   Heaven has no mouth but lets the people speak
       instead.   [J]

Western Equivalents

1926   Heaven [God] is above all.

1927   That which comes from above let no man question.

1928   God knows who's a good pilgrim.

1929   Man proposes, but God disposes.

1930   God [Heaven] helps them that help themselves.

1931   God never sendeth mouth but He sendeth meat.

1932   The voice of the people is the voice of God.

Fate: its power and effects

1933   Our destiny is fixed, without the slightest reference
       to our own will.   [C]

1934   Our destiny is in Heaven's hands.   [J]

[1921 – 1934]

1935   When marked out by destiny, a man will assuredly drown even though he lives his whole life among the highest branches of a date tree.   [C]

1936   Every event is settled beforehand; so it is vain to fret over this transitory life.   [C]

1937   Nothing follows man's own calculations; his whole life is arranged by his fate.   [C]

1938   Destiny has four feet, eight hands, and sixteen eyes; how then shall the ill-doers with only two of each hope to escape?   [C]

1939   Hide yourself in a pot, and yet you will never flee your fate.   [K]

1940   When a man's sleeve brushes another's, even that slight touch is predestined.   [K] [J]

1941   Whilst men sit in their houses, Heaven sends calamity upon them.   [C]

1942   Every man has his fate bound about his neck.   [J]

1943   A man can be cured of his illness, but there is no cure for his fate.   [C]

1944   Happiness and misery are not fated but self-gained.   [C]

1945   Men are good or bad according to their conduct; their misery or happiness depends on themselves.   [C]

[1935–1945]

Western Equivalents

1946 No flying from fate.

1947 That shall be, shall be.

1948 What must be, must be.

1949 The event is never in the power of man.

1950 Earth receives all that falls from Heaven.

1951 Fate leads the willing, and drags along those who hang back.

1952 No matter where an ox goes he must plow.

Fortune and misfortune: their nature and effects

1953 Success or failure in life is all determined by one's original fortune or misfortune.　　　　[K]

1954 Never think that fortune and misfortune are far from you forever.　　　　[J]

1955 There is a piece of fortune in misfortune.　　[J]

1956 Who knows this morning what will happen tonight?　　　　　　[C]

1957 One inch ahead is all darkness.　　　[K] [J]

1958 A man's fortune turns like a waterwheel.　[K]

1959 Fortunes never come in two's; misfortunes never come alone.　　　　[K] [J]

[1946 – 1959]

A man's fortune turns like a waterwheel.

1960   Out of luck, gold becomes iron; in luck, iron
resembles gold.   [C]

1961   Keep misfortune for three years, and it may turn
out to be of some use.   [J]

1962   After a rain the ground becomes firm.   [K] [J]

1963   Even a stranded dragon will one day ascend to the
sky.   [C]

[1960 – 1963]

1964   The sunbeam will stream even into a mousehole.
[K]

1965   Even the Yellow River has its clear days; how can man be altogether without luck? [C]

> † A day that the Yellow River's waters are clear is said to come once or twice in a millenium.

1966   Every grasshopper has his day in June. [K]

1967   Even the thistle's blossoms have a moment of full bloom. [J]

1968   Wherever good fortune visits a house, it is accompanied to the door by devils. [J]

1969   Great fortunes depend on luck; tiny fortunes depend on diligence. [C]

1970   Half of your fortune lies in your family line. [K]

Western Equivalents

1971   God sends good luck and God sends bad.

1972   You never know your luck.

1973   It chances in an hour, that happens not in seven years.

1974   Great fortune brings with it great misfortune.

1975   Misfortunes never come singly.

1976   The darkest hour is that before the dawn.

1977   Every cloud has a silver lining.

1978   Bad luck often brings good luck.

1979   After a storm comes a calm.

1980   Every dog has his day.

1981   Fortune knocks once at every man's gate.

1982   Better be born lucky than wise.

Luck: good and favorable

1983   Good luck comes like a large watermelon sitting in the middle of a freshly tidied room.   [C]

1984   Good luck is something you can look forward to while lying down at leisure.   [K]

1985   For good luck, sleep and wait.   [J]

1986   Waiting for good luck is like waiting for death.   [J]

1987   The dead tree has burst into blossom.   [K]

† This is said when a surprisingly great thing has happened to a worthless family.

1988   A rice cake has fallen down to a man sitting in the cellar.   [K]

† Someone has had incredibly good luck. The following two proverbs express the same.

1989   A rice cake has fallen down from the shelf.   [J]

[1977 – 1989]

1990   A pumpkin has fallen off its vine.   [K]

Western Equivalents

1991   Lucky men need no counsel.

1992   To think that larks will fall into one's mouth roasted.

1993   Good luck reaches further than long arms.

Luck: hard and bad

1994   Misfortune is not that which can be avoided, but that which cannot.   [C]

1995   Misfortune comes to all men and most women. [C]

1996   To lose one's father in youth, to lose one's wife in middle age, and to die without an heir, are the three greatest misfortunes.   [C]

1997   The three greatest misfortunes in one's life: a flood, a fire, and a bad wife.   [K]

1998   Illness goes in at the mouth; misfortune comes out of the mouth.   [C] [J]

1999   No sooner do you escape a deer than you come across a tiger.   [K]

† Some people are fated to meet with endless series of misfortunes.

2000   One calamity follows close on the heels of another.   [J]

2001 Whenever he peddles salt, it rains; whenever he peddles flour, the wind blows. [K]

2002 To bite on a bone in an egg. [K]

† This is said of a man who is prone to hard luck.

2003 The frost fallen upon the snow. [K]

† One misfortune follows another.

Western Equivalents

2004 Misfortunes find their way even on the darkest night.

2005 It never rains but it pours.

2006 Out of the frying pan into the fire.

2007 The bread never falls but on its buttered side.

2008 Ill comes often on the back of worse.

* * *

Heaven is under our feet as well as over our head.
— *Henry D. Thoreau*

0 fortune, fortune! All men call thee fickle.
— *Shakespeare*

2 DEVILS AND HELL

Devils: their nature and influence

2009   Many devils lurk in auspicious things and events.
[*J*]

2010   Whenever good fortune visits a house, it is
accompanied to the door by devils.   [*J*]

2011   The poorer one is, the more devils one meets.   [*C*]

2012   A man driven into a corner is apt to plot iniquity.
[*J*]

2013   Men do evil when they are idle.   [*J*]

2014   To help the tyrant in committing atrocities.   [*C*]

2015   Anticipating, and thereby instigating, the sovereign
to do evil.   [*C*]

   † According to Mencius, the crime of him who con-
nives at and aids the wickedness of his prince is
small, but the crime of him who anticipates and ex-
cites that wickedness is great.

2016   Thieves also have principles.   [*C*]

[2009 – 2016]

2017   Honor among thieves.   [C]

2018   Even among devils there are some Buddhas.   [J]

Western Equivalents

2019   The devil is never far off.

2020   The devil is at home.

2021   The devil is a busy bishop in his own diocese.

2022   The devil dances in an empty pocket.

2023   The devil finds work for idle hands.

2024   An idle brain is the devil's shop.

2025   The devil is not so black as he is painted.

2026   Hold a candle to the devil.

2027   Give the devil his due.

Heaven and hell

2028   Both Hell and Heaven exist in this world.   [J]

2029   Hell is just next door.   [J]

2030   Hell and Heaven both have their Quiet Land.   [C]
  † The "Quiet Land" means a place of rest and peace.

2031   In Hell the bottommost seats are reserved for the
       overlords.   [J]

† Feudal lords or their equivalents, who once mistreated their people on earth, will be subjected to severe punishment in Hell.

2032 **To take the road to Hell instead of the road to Heaven.** [**K**]

† This is said of someone who persistently does evil, never caring to seek opportunities to do good.

Western Equivalents

2033 **Hell is where heaven is not.**

2034 **Descent to Hell is easy.**

2035 **Hell is always open.**

2036 **Princes are venison in heaven.**

Hell is just next door.

*   *   *

The heart of man is the place the Devil's in: I feel
sometimes a Hell within myself.

— *Thomas Browne*

Hell is a city much like London.

— *P. B. Shelley*

3 SUPERSTITIONS

Diet and table manners: their effects

2037 **If you become a vegetarian, you separate from your
ancestors and cut off posterity.**   **[C]**

2038 **If you eat the eyeballs of fish, you will be absent at
your parent's deathbed.**   **[K]**

† It is considered a serious lack of filial piety not to
be present when one's parent breathes his or her last.
Thus, one should refrain from eating the eyeballs of
fish.

2039 **If you tap your rice bowl with your chopsticks,
you'll be poor to the last generation.**   **[C]**

2040 **If you lie down right after eating, you'll turn into an ox.** [*K*] [*J*]

> † This proverb is probably based on the known habits of cows and oxen, which lie down right after eating and chew their cud.

2041 **There is luck in leftovers.** [*J*]

If you lie down right after eating,
you'll turn into an ox.

Western Equivalents

2042   **Oysters are only in season in the R months.**

> † The R months are those that have the letter R in their name: January, February, March, April, September, October, November, and December. This proverb implies that one should not eat oysters in the summer months — May, June, July, and August — when oysters can go bad easily.

2043   **To eat an apple without first rubbing it, is to challenge the Evil One.**

2044   **Speak not of a dead man at the table.**

2045   **To speak of a usurer at the table mars the wine.**

2046   **It is bad luck to spill salt at the table.**

Body parts: their effects

2047   **If your eyes start twitching, bad luck is bound to follow.**   [C]

2048   **If your ear itches, somebody is gossiping about you.**
                                    [K]

2049   **If your ear itches, good things will come.**   [J]

2050   **Big feet, great luck.**   [C]

2051   **We all suppose felicity hangs from the tips of toes.**
                                    [C]

2052   A man with a big head has a good destiny.   [*J*]

2053   A person with a broad forehead will have good luck.   [*J*]

2054   A person with big ear lobes is lucky.   [*J*]

2055   A hairy man is virile.   [*J*]

2056   A curly-haired woman is amorous.   [*J*]

2057   Horns will grow on the head of a jealous woman.   [*J*]

† This proverb is based on an earlier superstition that a jealous woman could turn into a demon.

2058   People with curly hair and inturned teeth are often miserly and hard-hearted.   [*K*]

Western Equivalents

2059   A dimple on the chin, your living comes in; a dimple on the cheek, your living to seek.

2060   Cold hands, warm heart.

2061   A moist hand augurs an amorous nature.

2062   Blue eyes, true eyes.

2063   Carry an acorn and you will have good luck.

2064   To cut a baby's nails before it is a year old, will make it grow up a thief.

2065   Cutting nails on Friday or Saturday is bad luck.

2066   An itchy right hand means money is coming and an itchy left hand means money is slipping away.

2067   If you eat bread crumbs, your hair will curl.

Things domestic

2068   If descendants are in any unhappy condition, that's because their house or an ancestor's grave is inauspiciously situated.   [C] [K]

> † Even today in some parts of Asia the location and lay of a house or a grave is often determined through geomancy.

2069   If you give female names to boys and male names to girls, they will grow up in good health.   [K] [J]

> † The ancient people's strategy was to mislead and ward off the demons of disease and bad luck.

2070   Under each man's name lies his own fortune.   [C]

2071   If a man is beaten with a broomstick, he will not live three more years.   [J]

2072   If a broomstick or a chopstick breaks, it is a bad omen.   [J]

2073   If you step on a book, you'll meet with divine retribution.   [J]

2074   If you come upon a comb, step on it once before you pick it up.   [J]

† This is believed to drive out the evil spirit in the comb.

2075 The long-staying guest will leave if you stand a broom upside down. [*J*]

Western Equivalents

2076 When a house burns, another should not be built on the same spot. If so, this one will burn too.

2077 No girl should risk marriage with a man whose last name has the same initial as hers.

2078 If a woman marries without changing names, this gives her the ability to cure certain diseases (e.g., mumps, measles).

2079 A guest should not refold his napkin after eating. If he does, he will not be invited back by the host.

2080 Two knives and forks placed accidentally at a plate is a sign of company coming.

2081 Laying the knife and fork across each other on the plate is a bad omen.

2082 Throwing salt over the left shoulder will ward off bad luck.

Times and seasons

2083 The child born in the daytime resembles its father; the child born at night resembles its mother. [*J*]

2084　Do not sweep your house on New Year's morning.
　　　　　　　　　　　　　　　　　　　　　　　　　　[*J*]

　　　† This is a caution against sweeping out all the good
　　　luck in the house.

2085　If you cut your nails in the evening, you'll be visited
　　　by a burgler that night.　　　　　　　　　　　　[*K*]

2086　If you whistile at night, a burgler will break into
　　　your house.　　　　　　　　　　　　　　　　　[*K*]

2087　If you play with fire in the evening, you'll wet your
　　　bed that night.　　　　　　　　　　　　　　　[*K*]

2088　If you wash your hair on a rainy day, it will rain on
　　　the day of a great family event.　　　　　　　　[*K*]

2089　If you sleep with your socks on, you'll be absent at
　　　your parent's deathbed.　　　　　　　　　　　　[*J*]

2090　If you sweep your room at night, you will become
　　　poor.　　　　　　　　　　　　　　　　　　　[*J*]

2091　If you sleep with your nightgown turned inside out,
　　　you'll dream of your loved one.　　　　　　　　[*J*]

Western Equivalents

2092　Sweep the house with the broom in May, and
　　　you'll sweep the luck of the house away.

2093　Friday's hair, and Saturday's horn, goes to the devil
　　　on Monday morn.

2094 Friday the 13th is the day of misfortune.

† On this day and date some people refrain from undertaking anything of importance, some businesses postpone the concluding of deals, some will be suspicious of foods, particularly at restaurants, and some will avoid using it for a wedding.

2095 A growing moon and a flowing tide are lucky times to marry in.

2096 Marry in Lent, and you'll live to repent.

2097 If the sun shines through the apple trees on Christmas Day, there will be an abundant crop the following year.

Animals

2098 The unicorn, the phoenix, the tortoise, and the dragon are the four spiritually endowed creatures.
[C]

2099 Whenever ravens fly over your head, there must be before you some trouble to dread. [C]

2100 If crows caw, somebody will die. [K]

2101 The cawing of a crow presages some calamity. [J]

2102 It goes ill with the house if the hen cackles at daybreak. [K]

2103 If you kill a cat, it will haunt you and your family for seven generations. [J]

2104 If a magpie perches near your door, you will soon
have guests. [C]

2105 If you hear the magpie's song in the morning,
fortune will come; if you hear the crow's caw at
night, calamity lay ahead. [K]

Western Equivalents

2106 It is a sad house where the hen crows at daybreak.

2107 A rooster crowing in the middle of the night is an
omen of bad news.

2108 A whistling woman and crowing hen are neither fit
for God.

2109 The croaking raven bodes death.

2110 The screeching of an owl is a bad omen.

2111 To kill a spider is to bring rain or poverty.

2112 When ants are unusually busy, foul weather is at
hand.

*   *   *

Superstition is the religion of feeble minds.
— *Edmund Burke*

Superstition is the poetry of life; thus it does not
hurt a poet to be superstitious.
— *Goethe*

KEY WORDS AND CONCEPTS
Numbers refer to proverbs

WESTERN PROVERBS

Numbers refer to proverbs

A

A bad workman always blames his tools. 586
A beautiful face is a silent commendation. 1805
A bird in the hand is worth two in the bush. 1239

A bold heart is half the battle.   244

Absence makes the heart grow fonder.   1701

Absence sharpens love, presence strengthens it.   1702

Abundance of things engenders disdainfulness.   1088

A burnt child dreads the fire.   351

Accidents will happen in the best-regulated families.   742

A cloudy morning bodes a fair afternoon.   1504

A cold April gives bread and wine.   1536

A cool mouth, and warm feet, live long.   1159

A courtesy is a flower.   68

A crowd is not company.   1475

A dimple on the chin, your living comes in; a dimple on the cheek, your living to seek.   2059

A dry cough is the trumpeter of death.   1174

A dry summer never made a dear peck.   1555

Adversity makes a man wise, not rich.   405

A fair face cannot have a crabbed heart.   1793

A feather in the hand is better than a bird in the air.   1238

A fool may give a wise man counsel.   420

A forced kindness deserves no thanks.   660

A foul morning may turn to a fair day.   1878

A friend in need is a friend indeed.   1406

A friend is not so soon gotten as lost.   1414

After a rainy winter follows a fruitful spring.   1590

After a storm comes a calm.   1877, 1979

After dinner sit awhile, after supper walk a mile.   1156

After meat, mustard.   1013

A gaudy morning bodes a wet afternoon.   1503

A golden key opens every door.   1068

A good beginning, but a poor finish.   1650

A good beginning makes a good ending.   1645

A good conscience is a soft pillow.   231

A good example is the best sermon.   322

A good heart cannot lie.   19

A good heart conquers ill fortune.   18

A good life hath but few days, but a good name endureth forever.   1910

A good salad may be the prologue to a bad supper.   1652

A good winter brings a good summer.   1592

A green winter makes a fat churchyard.   1593

A growing moon and a flowing tide are lucky times to marry in. 2095

A guest should not refold his napkin after eating. If he does, he will not be invited back by the host. 2079

A hasty man never wants woe. 1031

A hedge between keeps friendship green. 1412

A house is a fine house when good folks are within. 37

A jackdaw always perches by another jackdaw. 1438

A kind word is like a spring day. 758

A little child weighs on your knee, a big one on your heart. 1302

A little labor, much health. 1151

A little learning is a dangerous thing. 339

All happiness is in the mind. 921

All men are fated to die. 1890

All that glitters is not gold. 1829

All things obey money. 1067

All who live must die, and none who die can renew their life on earth. 1895

A man has the choice to begin love, but not to end it. 138

A man in debt is caught in a net. 1216

A man is known by his friends. 1431

A man is known by the company he keeps. 1430

A man is well or woeful as he thinks himself so. 885

A man of words and not of deeds is like a garden full of weeds. 847

A man should keep from the blind and give to his kin. 1268

A man's mind is a dark mirror. 901

A man's mother is his other God. 1328

A man's praise in his own mouth stinks. 541

A man's studies pass into his character. 300

A May cold is a thirty-day cold. 1172

A May flood never did good. 1539

A moist hand augurs an amorous nature. 2061

A mother's love is best of all. 207, 1327

A mother's love never ages. 208, 1329

An angry man never wants woe. 435

An apple a day keeps the doctor away. 1155

An army marches on its stomach. 1135

An enemy to beauty is a foe to nature. 858

An English summer, two fine days and a thunderstorm. 1552

Anger begins with folly and ends with repentance. 433
Anger is a short madness. 444
An honest look covereth many faults. 1804
An idle brain is the devil's shop. 2024
An idle youth, a needy age. 1686
An ill-advised marriage is a spring of misfortune. 1382
An ill beginning, an ill ending. 1649
An itchy right hand means money is coming and an itchy left hand
    means money is slipping away. 2066
An oak is not felled at one stroke. 289
An occasion lost cannot be redeemed. 991
An ounce of mirth is worth a pound of sorrow. 936
An ounce of mother is worth a ton of priest. 1332
Anything is better than nothing. 1237
A pious youth, an old-age devil. 1765
Apparel makes the man. 1790
April showers bring forth May flowers. 1535
A quiet conscience sleeps through thunder. 232
A ragged coat may cover an honest man. 1127
A rooster crowing in the middle of the night is an omen of bad
    news. 2107
Art is long, life is short. 1856
A scalded cat fears cold water. 352
As for me, all I know is that I know nothing. 299
A small leak will sink a great ship. 1740
A snow year, a rich year. 1511
A soft answer turneth away wrath. 447
A straight stick is crooked in the water. 1197
As you sow, so you reap. 1626
A thing of beauty is a joy forever. 859
Autumn, the fairest season of the year. 1572
Avarice is the only passion that never ages. 482
A vaunter and a liar are near akin. 556
A watched pot never boils. 286
A whip for a fool, and a rod for a school, is always in good season.
    212
A whistling woman and crowing hen are neither fit for God. 2108
A wise head makes a closed mouth. 804
A wise man changes his mind, a fool never. 396, 892
A wise man may sometimes play the fool. 415
A wonder lasts but nine days. 819

A word and a stone let go cannot be called back.   777
A young physician fattens the churchyard.   1177
A young trooper should have an old horse.   1764

B

Bad luck often brings good luck.   1978
Bad news travels fast.   816
Be as just as a square and as mild as a lamb.   219
Beauty and folly are often companions.   866
Beauty draws more than oxen.   857
Beauty is in the eye of the beholder.   147
Beauty is only skin-deep.   864
Beauty may have fair blossoms, yet bitter fruit.   865
Beauty may have fair leaves, yet bitter fruit.   1834
Beauty opens locked doors.   856
Beggars' begs are bottomless.   484
Better an egg today than a hen tomorrow.   1241
Better a sparrow in the hand than a pigeon on the roof.   1240
Better be born lucky than wise.   1982
Better be the head of a dog than the tail of a lion.   1739
Better fill a man's belly than his eye.   1138
Better late than never.   1001
Better the foot slip than the tongue.   779
Between two stools you fall to the ground.   1015
Birds of a feather flock together.   1437
Birds once snared fear all bushes.   354
Blood is thicker than water.   1258
Blue are the faraway hills.   1839
Blue eyes, true eyes.   2062
Books and friends should be few but good.   1411
Bread is the staff of life.   1134
Bright rain makes fools fain.   617
Burn not your house to fright the mouse away.   688

C

Care brings grey hair.   1046
Care killed the cat.   1045
Carry an acorn and you will have good luck.   2063
Changing of words is the lightening of hearts.   760

D

Do on the hill as you would do in the hall. 69
Do well and have well. 31
Dress up a stick, and it does not appear to be a stick. 1794
Dust thou art, and unto dust shalt thou return. 1907
Dying is as natural as living. 1906

E

Eagles do not breed doves. 1623
Earth receives all that falls from Heaven. 1950
Earth's crammed with heaven, and every common bush afire with
    God. 1571
Easier said than done. 849
Easy to be wise after the event. 419
Empty vessels make the greatest sound. 560, 850
Envy eats nothing but its own heart. 457
Envy shoots at others, but wounds herself. 458
Even Homer sometimes nods. 720
Evening red and morning grey help the traveler on his way; eve-
    ning grey and morning red bring down rain upon his head. 1498
Every bean has its black. 723
Every cloud has a silver lining. 1977
Every dog has his day. 976, 1980
Every dog is a lion at home. 251
Every dog is valiant at his own door. 252
Every family has a skeleton in the cupboard. 1292
Every man for himself, and God for us all. 529
Every man has his faults. 722
Every man is nearest himself. 505
Every mile is two in winter. 1585
Every one has a skeleton in his closet. 726
Every shoe fits not every foot. 727
Everything has its seed. 1618
Everything is good in its season. 975
Example is better than precept. 321
Experience is the best teacher. 317
Experience is the mother of wisdom. 403

F

Fair face, foul heart. 1835

Fall not out with a friend for a trifle. 1415
Far fowls have fair feathers. 1838
Far from home, near thy harm. 1700
Fate leads the willing, and drags along those who hang back. 1951
Fear of death is worse than death itself. 1043
Feed by measure and defy the physician. 1154
Few words are best. 801
Fields have eyes, and woods have ears. 828
Fine feathers make fine birds. 1792
First creep, and then walk. 283
Follow virtue like its shadow. 30
Fools are wise after the event. 418
Fools bite one another, but wise men agree together. 395
Forewarned is forearmed. 378
Fortune knocks once at every man's gate. 1981
Four eyes see more than two. 1455
Friday's hair, and Saturday's horn, goes to the devil on Monday
   morn. 2093
Friday the 13th is the day of misfortune. 2094
Friends agree best at a distance. 1703
Friendship increases in visiting friends, but in visiting them seldom.
   1413
Fruit-bearing autumn. 1575

G

Give a clown your finger, and he will take your hand. 121
Give him an inch and he will take a yard. 122, 483
Give the devil his due. 2027
Go abroad and you'll hear of home. 818
God and parents and our masters can never be requited. 96, 1325
God [Heaven] helps them that help themselves. 1930
God knows who's a good pilgrim. 1928
God never sendeth mouth but He sendeth meat. 1931
God sends good luck and God sends bad. 1971
Gold goes in at any gate except heaven's. 1069
Good luck reaches further than long arms. 1993
Good words cost nothing, but are worth much. 759
Good words without deeds are rushes and reeds. 846
Gossiping and lying go together. 839
Go well clad, for a stake well dressed seems not to be so. 1795

I

If cold wind reaches you through a hole, say your prayers, and mind your soul. 1173

If red the sun begins his race, expect that rain will follow apace. 1500

If the blind lead the blind, both shall fall into the ditch. 620

If the counsel be good, no matter who gave it. 1760

If the sun goes pale to bed, 'twill rain tomorrow, it is said. 1501

If the sun shines through the apple trees on Christmas Day, there will be an abundant crop the following year. 2097

If two rainbows appear at one time, they presage rain to come. 1507

If you eat bread crumbs, your hair will curl. 2067

If you lie down with dogs, you will get up with fleas. 1436

If you run after two hares at once, you will catch neither. 487

If youth knew! If age only could! 1763

If you wish good advice, consult an old man. 1759

If wind follows sun's course, expect fair weather. 1508

Ill comes often on the back of worse. 2008

Ill news comes apace. 817

In choosing a wife, and buying a sword, we ought not to trust another. 1353

In excess, even nectar is poison. 700

Injuries we write in marble, kindness in dust. 508

In marriage the husband should have two eyes, and the wife but one. 1357

In the spring a young man's fancy lightly turns to thoughts of love. 1533

In too much dispute truth is lost. 1473

It chances in an hour, that happens not in seven years. 1973

It is a blind goose that comes to the fox's sermon. 622

It is a foolish sheep that makes the wolf his confessor. 621

It is a great point of wisdom to find out one's own folly. 394

It is a kindly act to help the fallen. 84

It is a proud horse that will not bear his own provender. 549

It is a sad house where the hen crows at daybreak. 2106

It is bad luck to spill salt at the table. 2046

It is comparison that makes men happy or miserable. 922, 1731

It is easier to bear the misfortune of others. 511

It is good fishing in troubled waters. 1480

It is good to be near of kin to land. 1263

It is good to learn at other men's cost. 323

It is natural to die, as to be born.   1905
It is no sin to sell dear, but a sin to give ill measure.   1200
It is the pace that kills.   1044
It is the riches of the mind only that make a man rich and happy.
   887
It is the sorry flock where the ewe bears the bell.   1384
It never rains but it pours.   2005
It's an ill bird that fouls its own nest.   1269
It's better to be first in a village than second in Rome.   1738
It's too late to shut the stable door after the horse has bolted.   1011
It takes two to make a quarrel.   1476

J

Jack would be a gentleman if he had money.   1072

K

Keep thy shop, and thy shop will keep thee.   1196
Keep your eyes wide open before marriage, and half shut afterward.
   1380
Keep your mouth shut and your ears open.   807
Kill not the goose that lays the golden egg.   495
Kindness comes of will, it cannot be bought.   50
Kindness is the noblest weapon to conquer with.   51
Kindness to the just is never lost, but kindness to the wicked is un-
   kindness to yourself.   123
Knowledge is folly, except grace guide it.   338
Knowledge is power.   297
Knowledge is the mother of all virtue; all vice proceeds from igno-
   rance.   296
Know thyself.   343
Know your opportunity.   986

L

Lack of money is the root of all evil.   1114
Laws grind the poor, and rich men rule the law.   1105
Laying the knife and fork across each other on the plate is a bad
   omen.   2081
Learning in the breast of a bad man is as a sword in the hand of a
   madman.   340

M

No sweet without sweat. 1681
Nothing ages so quickly as a kindness. 120
Nothing is as bold as a blind mare. 253
Nothing is impossible to a willing mind. 1685
Nothing so sure as death. 1891
No tree bears fruit in autumn that does not blossom in the spring.
  1577

O

Of fair things the autumn is fair. 1573
Old friends and old wine and old gold are best. 1409
Once bitten, twice shy. 355
One father is enough to govern one hundred sons, but not a hundred sons one father. 1330
One father is more than a hundred schoolmasters. 1331
One good turn deserves another. 34, 111
One hand washes the other. 1456
One hour today is worth two tomorrow. 1017
One ill word asks another. 780
One kindness is the price of another. 110
One may think who dares not speak. 903
One potter envies another. 461
One rotten apple spoils the barrel. 1432
One scabbed sheep will mar a whole flock. 1433
One woodcock does make a winter. 1584
Open confession is good for the soul. 234
Opportunity seldom knocks twice. 990
Our neighbor's cow gives more milk than ours. 1837
Out of sight, out of mind. 1697
Out of the frying pan into the fire. 2006
Oysters are only in season in the R months. 2042

P

Patience is a plaster for all sores. 268
Patience is a remedy for every grief. 271
Patience, time, and money accommodate all things. 266, 945, 1074
Patient men win the day. 269
Penny-wise and pound-foolish. 486

Personal beauty is a greater recommendation than any letter of recommendation. 1806

Physician, heal thyself. 741

Physicians kill more than they cure. 1175

Pity is akin to love. 52

Pity is but one remove from love. 53

Pity swells the tide of love. 54

Plain dealing is a jewel. 222

Please your eye and plague your heart. 876

Pleasure must be purchased with the price of pain. 1772

Poor men seek meat for their stomach; rich men stomach for their meat. 1100

Poverty breeds strife. 1119

Poverty is no vice, but an inconvenience. 1116

Poverty is the most deadly and prevalent of all diseases. 1115

Poverty is the mother of crime. 1113

Poverty keeps together more homes than it breaks up. 1126

Poverty wants many things, but covetousness all. 481

Praise fills not the belly. 1243

Praise is not pudding. 1242

Praise the child, and you make love to its mother. 166

Praise without profit puts little in the pot. 1244

Prettiness dies first. 873

Prevention is better than cure. 381

Pride goeth before destruction, and a haughty spirit before a fall. 538

Pride had rather go out of the way than go behind. 547

Pride increases our enemies, but puts our friends to flight. 540

Pride is a flower that grows in the devil's garden. 539

Pride often wears the cloak of humility. 573

Pride will spit in pride's face. 548

Princes are venison in heaven. 2036

R

Real friendship does not freeze in winter. 1407

Red clouds in the east, rain the next day. 1502

Red sky at night, shepherd's delight; red sky in the morning, shepherd's warning. 1499

Relatives are friends from necessity. 1296

Remember you are but a man. 570

Summer has set in with its usual severity. 1551
Summer is a seemly time. 1549
Summer's parching heat. 1550
Summer will not last forever. 1554
Sunny winter, a plentiful harvest. 1591
Sweep the house with the broom in May, and you'll sweep the luck
  of the house away. 2092
Sweet is pleasure after pain. 1776
Swine, women, and bees cannot be turned. 661

T

Take away the cause and the effect will cease. 1622
Take not a musket to kill a butterfly. 687
Take the goods the gods provide. 992
Talent above talent. 1732
Talking to the wall. 663
Talk much, err much. 778
Talk of the donkey, and it will come trotting up. 831
Tell not all you know, all you have, or all you can do. 808
That shall be, shall be. 1947
That which comes from above let no man question. 1927
The best doctors are Dr. Diet, Dr. Quiet, and Dr. Merryman.
  1150
The best horse needs breaking, and the aptest child needs teaching.
  213
The best mirror is an old friend. 1408
The best of men are but men at best. 572
The best smell is bread, the best savor salt, the best love that of
  children. 1322
The bird is known by his note, the man by his words. 756
The birth follows the belly. 1261
The book of the heart is read from the eyes. 908
The borrower is servant to the lender. 1215
The bread never falls but on its buttered side. 2007
The burden is light on the shoulder of another. 510
The croaking raven bodes death. 2109
The crutch of time does more than the club of Hercules. 949
The customer is always right. 1194
The darkest hour is that before the dawn. 1876, 1976
The devil dances in an empty pocket. 1117, 2022

The voice of the people is the voice of God. 1932

The ways to enrich are many, and most of them foul. 1089

The wife is the key of the house. 1359

The wind in one's face makes one wise. 404

The world is for him who waits. 270

The worst wheel of a cart creaks most. 851

They can do least who boast loudest. 558

They die well that live well. 36

They must hunger in frost that will not work in heat. 1687

Things are not as black as they look. 1042

Things past cannnot be recalled. 966

Those who live in glass houses should not throw stones. 601

Three helping one another, bear burthen of six. 1454

Throwing salt over the left shoulder will ward off bad luck. 2082

Time and straw make medlars ripe. 978

Time and tide wait for no man. 965

Time cures all things. 946

Time devours all things. 950

Time flees away without delay. 964

Time flies. 961

Time has wings. 962

Time is a great healer. 948

Time is money. 944

To be loved, be lovable. 169

To be stabbed in the back. 522

To bite the hand that feeds you. 523

To build castles in the air. 669

To buy and sell, and live by the loss. 1199

To cut a baby's nails before it is a year old, will make it grow up a thief. 2064

To eat an apple without first rubbing it, is to challenge the Evil One. 2043

To err is human; to forgive divine. 728

To kill a spider is to bring rain or poverty. 2111

To live like Darby and Joan. 1355

To make a mountain out of a molehill. 561, 684

To make an elephant out of a fly. 685

Too far east is west. 701

Too many cooks spoil the broth. 1472

Too much of ought is good for nought. 699

To see no farther than the end of one's nose. 345

To sit on pins and needles. 287
To speak of a usurer at the table mars the wine. 2045
To start off with a bang and to end with a whimper. 689, 1651
To teach a dog to chase rabbits. 666
To teach a fish how to swim. 665
To teach the Pope how to pray. 667
To think that larks will fall into one's mouth roasted. 1992
To those in love miles are only paces. 133
Travel broadens the mind. 320
Trouble brings experience and experience brings wisdom. 406
Two cats and a mouse, two wives in one house, two dogs and a
    bone, never agree in one. 1477
Two daughters and a back door are three arrant thieves. 1298
Two dogs strive for a bone, and a third runs away with it. 1479
Two hands are better than one. 1453
Two is company, three is none. 1474
Two knives and forks placed accidentally at a plate is a sign of
    company coming. 2080
Two sparrows on one ear of corn make an ill agreement. 1478
Two things a man should never be angry at: what he can help, and
    what he cannot help. 448
Two things do prolong thy life: a quiet heart and a loving wife.
    1352

U

Under water, famine; under snow, bread. 1512

V

Valor is the nobleness of the mind. 242
Virtue and a trade are the best portion for children. 16
Virtue is a jewel of great price. 15
Virtue is its own reward. 32
Virtue is the beauty of the mind. 14
Virtue is the only true nobility. 17

W

Wake not a sleeping lion. 377
Walls have ears. 827

War, hunting, and love are as full of trouble as pleasure. 182
Weigh justly and sell dearly. 1201
We learn by doing. 318
Well begun is half done. 1646
Well kens the mouse when the cat's out of the house. 1710
We must learn to walk before we can run. 284
What escapes the eyes is no longer in the heart. 1699
What is man but his mind? 883
What is not wisdom is danger. 375
What must be, must be. 1948
What the fool does in the end, the wise man does at the start. 417
When a house burns, another should not be built on the same spot.
   If so, this one will burn too. 2076
When a man gets angry, his reason rides out. 432
When angry, count ten before you speak; if very angry, a hundred.
   446
When ants are unusually busy, foul weather is at hand. 2112
When fern grows red, then milk is good with bread. 1574
When fortune smiles, embrace her. 989
When friends meet, hearts warm. 1405
When poverty comes in at the door, love flies out of the window.
   1118
When the cat's away the mice will play. 1709
When the cuckoo comes, he eats up all the dirt. 1528
When the goodman is from home, the goodwife's table is soon
   spread. 1356
When the heart is full the tongue will speak. 906
When the mist comes from the hill, then good weather it doth spill;
   when the mist comes from the sea, then good weather it will be.
   1506
When the sun rises, the disease will abate. 1157
When the wind is in the west, the weather is at its best. 1510
When you can tread on nine daisies at once, spring has come. 1530
When you enter a house, leave your anger ever at the door. 445
Where bees are, there is honey. 1679
Where there are reeds, there is water. 837, 1620
Where there is peace, God is. 233
Where there is whispering, there is lying. 838
Where there's a will, there's a way. 1684
Where there's smoke, there's a fire. 836
Where the sun enters, the doctor does not. 1158